D1448841

THE HATTERS OF
EIGHTEENTH-CENTURY
FRANCE

THE HATTERS OF EIGHTEENTH-CENTURY FRANCE

MICHAEL SONENSCHER

University of California Press
Berkeley · Los Angeles · London

University of California Press
Berkeley and Los Angeles, California

University of California Press, Ltd.
London, England

© 1987 by
The Regents of the University of California

Library of Congress Cataloging-in-Publication Data
Sonenscher, Michael.
  The hatters of eighteenth-century France.

  Bibliography: p.
  Includes index.
  1. Hatters—France—History—18th century.
2. Compagnonnages. 3. Labor and laboring classes—
France—History—18th century. I. Title.
HD8039.H32F77 1987   331.7′6874′0944   86-11431
ISBN 0-520-05827-5

Printed in the United States of America

1 2 3 4 5 6 7 8 9

I fancy mankind may come, in time,
to write all aphoristically, except in narrative;
grow weary of preparation and connection
and illustration, and all those arts by which
a big book is made.

Samuel Johnson, in James Boswell,
Journal of a Tour to the Hebrides (London, 1785)

Contents

vii

Abbreviations and Units of Measurement

A.C.	Archives communales
A.D.	Archives départementales
A.N.	Archives nationales (Paris)
B.H.V.P.	Bibliothèque historique de la ville de Paris
B.M.	Bibliothèque municipale
B.N.	Bibliothèque nationale (Paris)

As is customary, I have retained the original orthography in citing archival sources. Punctuation and accents have, however, been modernized.

The standard unit of currency in eighteenth-century France was the livre. One livre was made up of 20 sous and one sou (or sol) was made up of 12 deniers. The écu was worth 3 livres and the louis was worth 6 livres.

Unless otherwise specified all weights are denominated in Parisian pounds and ounces. A pound in eighteenth-century Paris was equivalent to 489.5 grams. A hundred pounds was known as a quintal.

Preface

Despite its epigraph, this essay is a narrative of a conventional sort. It is an account of what happened in a trade in France during the eighteenth century. In an oblique way it is also a contribution to a broader discussion of the relationship between work and politics. The meaning of the terms is now very much more blurred than might have been the case fifteen or twenty years ago. They have a broader, more open-ended sense. Work is no longer defined solely as work for wages; politics are no longer confined to parties and policies. Most forms of work, whether for wages or not, entail various kinds of cooperation and negotiation between social unequals. This essay is a study of those processes within an eighteenth-century French trade. The history of how hats were made is, in this sense, also the history of a political culture.

Arguments over rights and obligations take many different forms. Historians of early modern Europe have associated the subject mainly with questions of religious affiliation or with matters related to the land and rights to the use of the land. One effect of this entirely understandable preoccupation has been that the ordinary inhabitants of towns and cities have been consigned to a historiographical limbo inhabited mainly by crowds (or mobs) whose rituals and culture are always "popular," "customary," or "traditional." One of the aims of this essay is to show that, even though eighteenth-century French hatters may have belonged to crowds or participated in mobs—and (like bankers and lawyers) had their own distinctive beliefs—they also inhabited the same cultural world as writers of high political theory and authors of austere treatises of civil jurisprudence.

The work of making hats did not simply happen. It was a process of negotiation conducted within the changing terms of reference of the culture of the wider polity. As that culture changed, the tension between the rights of producers and the rights of society became sharper. Identities and practices that were once the subject of legal argument became a series of apparently archaic customs and traditions. In doing so, they acquired some of the features of what might seem to have been a distinctively artisanal culture. They are, however, better understood in the context of the shifting relationship between public obligations and private arrangements. The apparently custom-bound world of a pre-industrial society was the product of a political history in which the law and the decisions of the courts played a significant part.

This emphasis upon the importance of the law in the life of an eighteenth-century trade also means—and in an equally oblique way—that this essay is an attempt to approach the politics of the French Revolution from a different point of view. The historiography of the Revolution has come to resemble an old armchair, offering a familiar invitation to commemoration or disputation. Yet even old armchairs were once made, and made from very disparate materials. The history of a single trade may not be the best place to find many of these materials. Yet some of them, particularly the things that people said and did when they went to court and used the law, were part of the public life of eighteenth-century France. They were also very much a part of the history of how hats were made. As a result, that history offers a vantage point for a closer examination of argument over the ordinary uses of power in urban France before the Revolution. The words used in 1789 and thereafter had resonances that are perhaps best understood in the context of the forgotten dramas of the everyday world of the eighteenth century.

This study was originally a chapter in a more extensive study of the urban trades of eighteenth-century France. As sometimes happens, it became a little too long to be included in that work. It also became clear that the narrative form of this account was best presented separately, so that some of the themes broached here could be developed more extensively in their own right elsewhere. Information on specific trades in eighteenth-century France (apart from the textile trades) is not particularly easy to find. Despite many hopes, I was not able to find a set of business records that would have allowed me to make precise calculations of costs, profits, wages, earnings, or short-term changes in patterns of employment in a quantitative or serial manner. Like most historians I have had to make do with what there is. A brief note at the end of this study provides an outline of the principal sources I have used. I hope that it may be of use to other historians because, despite the fragmentary nature of the sources, there is much to be found.

I am grateful to the many archivists and librarians in Paris, Lyon, Marseille, Nîmes, Rouen, Rennes, Toulouse, Geneva, and Brussels whose collections have formed the basis of this essay. I am grateful too to Professor William Eccles of the University of Toronto for answering my questions on the Canadian fur trade with France. I would not have been able to collect the material cited here without the financial support of the British Economic and Social Research Council, the British Academy, the Twenty-Seven Foundation, the Nuffield Foundation, and the Middlesex Polytechnic. My time in France was made the more enjoyable thanks to the generous hospitality of Marc and Anne-Marie Lefèvre, Christian Hoc, Jean-Pierre and Michèle Hirsch, Feruccio Gambino, and Giovanna Procacci. The late Jacqueline Marchand was also a kind host during many of my visits to Paris. Parts of this study were presented to seminars at the University of Warwick and the European University Institute in Florence. I am grateful to Maxine Berg and Carlo Poni for their invitations and to the people who attended for their comments. I am particularly indebted to Colin Jones and Steven Kaplan for their observations on an earlier draft of the text and to the anonymous readers whose very helpful criticisms and suggestions were sent to the publishers of this book when it was under consideration. The faults that remain in the text are entirely my responsibility. I am grateful to Alison Shepherd of the Middlesex Polytechnic and Kate MacFarlane for the illustrations in the text and to Beverly Chapman and her colleagues of the Middlesex Polytechnic Library for much help and many acts of kindness. I would also like to thank Vanessa Chadwick and Linda Grant, who once spent part of a summer typing a thesis that has no connection with this work but whose completion allowed me to begin the project that led to this essay (for such are the requirements of more modern forms of entitlement). Sheila Levine, Betsey Scheiner, and Rose Vekony organized the production of this work with great clarity, skill, and efficiency. Thanks to Miles Taylor for help with the proofs. I am grateful too to Elizabeth Allen and to Kate, Luke, Radegund, and Joel Norbury for most of what I have learned about rights and obligations in everyday life.

1

The Price of a Day's Work

We do not know much about the work that people did before the emergence of mechanized systems of production. Although there are a number of studies of artisans—and the question of the relationship between artisanal production, popular politics, and the process of industrialization in the eighteenth and early nineteenth centuries is a subject of wide historical interest—we remain largely ignorant of what happened when people worked.[1] This is a study of what happened when people made hats.

Making a hat was not just a technical process. It was also the product of certain assumptions about the meaning of the work itself.[2] Throughout the eighteenth and early nineteenth centuries, journeymen in the French hatting trade

1. For an introduction to the problem, see Maurice Godelier, "Work and Its Representations: A Research Proposal," *History Workshop Journal* 10 (1980): 164–74. The classics are E. P. Thompson, *The Making of the English Working Class* (London, 1963), and E. J. Hobsbawm, *Labouring Men* (London, 1964). See also John Rule, *The Experience of Labour in Eighteenth-Century Industry* (London, 1981); Iorwerth Prothero, *Artisans and Politics in Early Nineteenth-Century London* (London, 1979); Robert D. Storch, ed., *Popular Culture and Custom in Nineteenth-Century England* (London, 1982); Maxine Berg, *The Age of Manufactures, 1700–1820* (London, 1985); and, on France, William Sewell, *Work and Revolution in France: The Language of Labor from the Old Regime to 1848* (London, 1980); William J. Reddy, *The Rise of Market Culture: The Textile Trade and French Society, 1750–1900* (London, 1984); Steven L. Kaplan and Cynthia J. Koepp, eds., *Work in France: Representations, Meaning, Organization, and Practice* (Ithaca, 1986).

2. Here ethnographers have made a major contribution. The questions posed in this study owe much to Clifford Geertz, *The Interpretation of Cultures* (New York, 1973) and *Local Knowledge* (New York, 1983). See also Pierre Bourdieu, *Outline of a Theory of Practice* (London, 1977); Marshall Sahlins, *Culture and Practical Reason* (Chicago, 1976); Hans Medick and David Warren Sabean, eds., *Interest and Emotion* (London, 1984).

refused to make more than two hats a day. This is a study of why they did so.

In a sense work never tells its own story. Like the genetic codes transmitted in the reproduction of living organisms, work carries images and aphorisms of the wider nexus of social life within its own cadences and rhythms.[3] The reason why work was done in certain ways in different times and places does not belong entirely to the techniques deployed in the work itself. To understand what happened when people made hats in eighteenth-century France, the essential prerequisites to an understanding of a trade—materials and skills, costs and profits, products and markets—need to be placed within a wider context of meaning. As a result, the story that work has to tell is also, and perhaps most fundamentally, the story of a political culture. The best way to understand what happened when hats were made in eighteenth-century France is to read Grotius, Pufendorf, Barbeyrac, and Burlamaqui.

It is, of course, unlikely that many of the people directly involved in making hats were particularly familiar with their works, or with those of the host of less celebrated authors of treatises of civil jurisprudence published during the eighteenth century.[4] In an indirect way, however, the body of

3. For one model series of studies, see Gerald M. Sider, "Christmas Mumming and the New Year in Outport Newfoundland," *Past and Present* 71 (1976): 102–25; "The Ties That Bind: Culture and Agriculture, Property and Propriety in the Newfoundland Village Fishery," *Social History* 5 (1980): 1–39; "Family Fun in Starve Harbour: Custom, History, and Confrontation in Village Newfoundland," in Medick and Sabean, eds., *Interest*, 340–70. See also Gerald M. Sider, *Culture and Class in Anthropology and History: A Newfoundland Illustration* (London, 1986).

4. What follows is a synthetic summary of Jean Domat, *Les Lois civiles dans leur ordre naturel*, 3 vols. (Paris, 1689–94), which went through sixty-four editions during the eighteenth century (see René-Frédéric Voeltzel, *Jean Domat (1625–1696): Essai de reconstitution de sa philosophie juridique, précédé de la biographie du jurisconsult* [Paris, 1936]). I have used the 1835 edition (see especially 199–200, "Du louage"). See also in the same edition Domat's *Le Droit public*, especially 236. Pufendorf's *De jure naturae et gentium* was translated by Jean Barbeyrac as *Le Droit de la nature et des gens*, 2 vols. (Amsterdam, 1706). I have also relied on H. Prévost de la Jannès, *Les Principes de la jurisprudence française*, 2 vols. (Paris, 1750); J. Réal de Courban, *La*

legal and political theory associated with what has come to be known as the natural law tradition supplied part of the ordinary vocabulary used in daily negotiation in the eighteenth-century French trades.[5] In the hatting trade its terms and propositions served to define the wage relationship in a certain way and supplied much of the substance of the formal identities that were brought into play in the work of making hats.

Journeymen in the eighteenth-century French hatting trade worked for wages. The words used to describe the wages they earned had a very precise sense. Two terms were used most frequently. The first, which applied to men paid at a daily rate, was *le prix d'une journée*, the price of a day's work. The second, which applied to men (and women) paid by the piece, was *le prix de la façon*, the price of making the article in question.[6] In both cases, the formal identity of the wage rela-

---

Science du gouvernement, 8 vols. (Paris and Amsterdam, 1764); and R. J. Pothier, *Traité du contrat de louage* (Orleans, 1768). I have used the 1820 edition of J. J. Burlamaqui, *Principes du droit de la nature et des gens* (3:273, "Du contrat de louage"), published originally in Yverdon, 1767–68. The secondary literature on these authors is not particulary distinguished. One of the best guides remains Robert Derathé, *Jean-Jacques Rousseau et la science politique de son temps* (Paris, 1950). See also Nannerl O. Keohane, *Philosophy and the State in France* (Princeton, 1980). Some indication of the continuing importance of the natural law tradition in eighteenth-century intellectual life can be found in Duncan Forbes, *Hume's Philosophical Politics* (London, 1975), 3–58; Robert M. Cover, *Justice Accused: Antislavery and the Judicial Process* (New Haven, 1975), 1–41; the editors' introduction to Istvan Hont and Michael Ignatieff, eds., *Wealth and Virtue: The Shaping of Political Economy in the Scottish Enlightenment* (London, 1983); and, in connection with civic and utilitarian modes of political argument, J. G. A. Pocock, *Virtue, Commerce, and History* (London, 1985). My thinking on the subject has been heavily influenced by Richard Tuck, *Natural Rights Theories* (London, 1979), which, although it is not directly concerned with any of the writers listed above, is a model application of historical intelligence to difficult and archaic texts.

    5. Many other examples of the use of this vocabulary will be presented in Michael Sonenscher, *Work and Wages in Eighteenth-Century France* (forthcoming); see also Sonenscher, "Weavers, Wage-Rates, and the Measurement of Work in Eighteenth-Century Rouen," *Textile History* 17 (1986): 7–18, and "Journeymen, the Courts, and the French Trades, 1781–1791," *Past and Present* 114 (1987).

    6. For examples of this usage, see A.N. X^{1b} 4232 (28 April 1785); 4236 (22 June 1785). See also the *arrêts* cited below, pp. 99–101.

tionship was analogous to the lease of goods or services. Just as one might pay a fee for the use of a coach or a plow, so the wage was the price paid for the use of someone else's capacity to work. Work for wages was, in formal terms, identical to the lease of property.[7] In this case, however, the property in question was labor.

This assimilation of labor to property was one of the distinguishing features of eighteenth-century French civil jurisprudence. In England a combination of statute and common law meant that the word "servant" (as in master and servant legislation) had a very wide range of connotations until well into the nineteenth century.[8] In France the word had a more limited formal meaning. Journeymen were not servants and, unless the law ruled otherwise, they were free to dispose of their labor as they chose.[9] This was because property in labor was a natural right. In France the notion of natural rights played an important part in a wider series of arguments about the nature of society and civil obligation whose history was coextensive with the history of absolutist gov-

7. "Toutes ces espèces de conventions ont cela de commun, qu'en chacune l'un jouit de la chose de l'autre, ou use de son travail pour un certain prix, et c'est pour cette raison que dans le droit romain elles sont toutes comprises sous les noms de louage et de conduction." Domat, *Lois civiles,* 199–200. "Le louage donc en général est un contrat par lequel l'un donne à l'autre, moyennant un certain loyer ou un salaire, l'usage et la jouissance d'une chose ou de son travail et de son industrie pour un certain temps." Burlamaqui, *Principes* 3:273.

8. D. Simon, "Master and Servant," in John Saville, ed., *Democracy and the Labour Movement* (London, 1954), 160–200; D. C. Woods, "The Operation of the Master and Servants Act in the Black Country, 1858–1875," *Midland History* 7 (1982): 93–115. I am aware that the contrast that I have made may be somewhat overdrawn. There is, however, no adequate study of the law in the life of the eighteenth-century trades in Britain.

9. "Le compagnonage [*sic*] est libre, et au choix de l'apprentif devenu compagnon, qui peut s'engager sous quel maître et dans quelle boutique il lui plaît." Jacques Savary des Bruslons, *Dictionnaire universel de commerce,* 2 vols. (Paris, 1723), 1:1433, s.v. "Compagnon." This liberty could be (and was) limited considerably by corporate statute or deliberation. It is important to bear in mind, however, that even though restrictions of this kind occurred very widely, they retained an exceptional character in legal terms.

ernment.[10] This body of argument—"a pile of tedious and indigestible erudition," in the words of one of its critics—formed the tradition of natural law.[11] Many of the assumptions used in argument over the identity and significance of natural rights and natural law were also the basis of legal provisions affecting the trades for much of the eighteenth century.

In the natural law tradition labor was a form of property because it was a natural human attribute like life, liberty, or reason. Men had property in their labor just as they had property in their lives or their liberty. They could alienate that labor voluntarily, just as they could alienate their liberty voluntarily. The price of the voluntary alienation of labor was the wage; the price of the voluntary alienation of natural liberty was the rule of law. *In*voluntary alienation of either labor or liberty, however, was slavery. In the natural law tradition, labor—like liberty or reason—was one of those singular qualities that distinguished humanity from the rest of God's creation. This emphasis upon natural human qualities was, of course, what separated writers in the natural law tradition, like Grotius, Pufendorf, Domat, or Pothier, from their better-known eighteenth-century critics. The natural law tradition was, in this sense, the other side of the Enlightenment. Since argument over natural law and natural rights played a part both in defining the wage relationship and in the wider sphere of civil litigation in the eighteenth-century French trades, it is essential to understand how the assumptions underpinning the natural law tradition differed from those deployed by its enlightened critics.

The difference between the two traditions is best summa-

10. For an outline of this relationship, see Tuck, *Natural Rights*. The most celebrated exponent of the natural rights argument was, of course, Thomas Hobbes. To my knowledge there is no adequate study of the role of Hobbes in eighteenth-century French intellectual life.

11. Simon Linguet, *Théorie des lois civiles* (Paris, 1767). I have used the reprinted edition of 1984 (published by Fayard in Paris). The words in question—"un amas d'érudition indigeste et assommante" (p. 58)—were directed at Grotius in particular.

rized in one of those paradoxical assertions that were a hall-mark of eighteenth-century debate and that contemporaries recognized as one of Rousseau's most durable legacies.[12] In his *Théorie des lois civiles* (1767), the lawyer Simon Linguet began a discussion of the origin of laws with the assertion that it was society that produced laws and not laws that had produced society.[13] The formulation marks the distance be-tween the natural law tradition, as embodied in the work of someone like the jurist Jean Domat, and its enlightened or utilitarian counterpart, as expounded by Linguet. Laws, for someone like Linguet, were the product of specific forms of civil society. Civil society, for someone like Domat, was the product of certain conventions that entitled those who made them to rights of particular kinds.

For much of the eighteenth century, civil jurisprudence derived from the premises of the tradition of natural law. Laws produced society; society was therefore a composite compound of voluntary conventions. The voluntaristic con-ception of civil society that was the hallmark of the natural law tradition meant that civil rights were exceptional in char-acter and could also be described as privileges (the word is, of course, derived from the Latin *lex privata*). Civil rights were titles, or formal entitlements, conferred upon particular individuals or collectivities in exchange for surrendering their natural rights to the safekeeping of the sovereign au-thority. In the jurisprudence of eighteenth-century France, civil rights pertained to particular groups of people—or towns, regions, or trades—rather than to society as a whole. The civil law embodied the particular needs and concerns of the multiplicity of different people who had entered into a rule-bound social existence by surrendering their universal natural rights to the custody of an absolute sovereign, the king.

12. See, for example, comments on the *Nouvelle Héloïse* published in R. A. Leigh, ed., *Correspondance complète de Jean-Jacques Rousseau*, vol. 8 (Ge-neva and Madison, 1969), such as "Cet auteur veut aller à la Postérité à force de paradoxes & de Séduction" (p. 59).

13. Linguet, *Théorie*, 107.

The exceptional and finite character of civil rights explains the apparent particularism of the orders, estates, corporations, and other privileged bodies of eighteenth-century French public life. That particularism was a cultural rather than a material phenomenon. For civil rights were only the most visible form of the wider array of natural rights whose claims had been modified and limited by their alienation to the absolute sovereign, the king. The corporate liberties of the eighteenth-century French polity are intelligible only in the context of a tradition of civil jurisprudence in which the transfer of natural rights and obligations to an absolute sovereign power was the basis of civil titles of different kinds.[14] Natural rights did not therefore disappear. They had been transferred to the custody of the absolute sovereign. The particularistic character of civil rights was matched by a recognition that natural rights could be invoked by appealing to the sovereign to whom they had been transferred. This was why the eighteenth-century French monarchy was, above all, a judicial institution and why the royal courts, and the Parlements in particular, played a central part in adjudicating between the respective claims of natural and civil rights.

A corporation like the hatters' corporation of eighteenth-century Paris was, from this perspective, a collective body that had been granted a title by the king to govern its own affairs in exchange for its recognition of his sovereign authority. The terms of that title were laid down in its statutes. They had been drafted by lawyers; examined by magistrates (in this case the *lieutenant général de police* and *procureur du roi* of the Châtelet of Paris); issued in the form of royal letters patent and ratified, after further scrutiny, by the Parlement of Paris. Similar procedures governed the naming of civil

---

14. In this I diverge somewhat from Sewell, *Work and Revolution*. What he has described as a "corporate idiom" was also a component of a wider tradition of civil jurisprudence that is absent from his book. The two interpretations are not incompatible, but they do give rise to somewhat different characterizations of both the culture of French artisans and the identity of revolutionary politics and their aftermath. My argument will be presented at much greater length in *Work and Wages*.

rights and obligations in most trades and cities. The magistrates or the Parlements were different (for they too had titles and rights of various kinds), but the procedures were the same. Corporations, like other individual and collective legal agents, enjoyed limited rights of an exceptional character because they had transferred their natural rights to the custody of the king and his courts.

Civil rights were titles to a public identity. They expressed the voluntary and contractual nature of civil association. They were therefore in the possession (as lawyers put it) of those individuals or groups whose natural rights had been surrendered to the custody of the absolute sovereign in exchange for the limited rights conferred by the law. As a result, civil rights were infinitely various. They met the different needs of those who possessed them. The rights of bakers and hatters, for example, were not the same because they made different things and served different needs. Yet this diversity was never stable. It offered a permanent invitation to comparison: between one locality and another, between one time and another, and between one set of legal entitlements and another. The heterogeneity of legal titles was, in this way, the ground upon which argument over rights and obligations was conducted. Corporate statutes, like any civil title, could be challenged in the courts. They had no absolute character. The rights they embodied were variants upon a range of different civil rights embodied in other titles.

Litigation in eighteenth-century France took several different forms. In one form it could entail argument and counter-argument over the legitimacy or relevance of particular actions or decisions in the light of the provisions of statutory titles. Many disputes between master artisans took this form.[15] Here precedent and counter-precedent played a

15. For one example, see the protracted dispute over the financial administration of the hatters' corporation of Lyon between 1743 and 1751, A.N. X^{1b} 3572 (7 October 1747); 3584 (31 August 1748); 3614 (24 October 1750); 3616 (11 January 1751); 7879 (11 December 1743); 7961 (21 August 1748); 7998 (28 November 1750).

significant part in legal argument. That was why corporate bodies maintained archives containing titles many hundreds of years old. The past was one of the keys to the content and extent of rights claimed in the present. Demonstration of possession—or, inversely, of the irrelevance of a rival claim to possession—was a necessary prerequisite to the exercise of a legal title.

Since civil rights were titles of a limited kind, legal argument could also take other forms. Where the law was silent it was possible to invoke the natural rights to which everyone was entitled. A Parisian journeyman hatter who walked out on his employer in 1721 readily agreed that he had violated the provisions of the corporation's statutes by failing to give his master a month's notice, but he denied that he was required to have a certificate attesting to the satisfactory completion of his work before he could be employed elsewhere.[16] Neither he nor anyone else in the trade had ever been subjected (*assujettis*) to any requirement to obtain a certificate, he stated. Unless the law ruled otherwise (as it did on the question of a period of notice), journeymen were free to dispose of their labor as they chose.

As this incident implies, journeymen were also able to challenge the provisions of the law. Although they had no formal corporate identity (and could be challenged in their turn if they embarked upon legal actions under a collective name), the limited and exceptional character of civil rights meant that it was possible to question titles that, it could be argued, violated journeymen's collective natural or civil rights. Corporate decisions affecting journeymen in a general way (such as a requirement to carry a certificate of good conduct or changes in modes of wage payment) were modifications of established rights. Like any such modification they required the sanction of the courts. Decisions by the corporations were, for this reason, subject to the same process of scrutiny and ratification as were their original titles to a civil identity. They could, for the same reason, also be

16. A.N. Y 14 932 (13 November 1721), deposition of Jacques Langlois.

opposed on the grounds that they established obligations that exceeded rights already embodied in the wording of statutory titles. The civil law in eighteenth-century France was a porous medium that allowed individuals or groups with common interests to challenge legal decisions by mounting collective actions in the courts despite the absence of a formal public identity.

At various times during the eighteenth century, journeymen in the hatting trade combined to hire solicitors and barristers to challenge corporate decisions in the courts. In this they were by no means unusual.[17] The arguments they used varied from issue to issue, but their status as litigants remained intact for much of the eighteenth century. For as long as the law remained a composite body, consisting of a range of heterogeneous titles whose provisions were designed to match the various needs of different social groups, civil rights were finite and particular in character. Only when the law acquired a simpler, more universal character—and civil rights and obligations came to be defined as ends in themselves rather than as modifications or exceptions to natural rights—did the notion of rights of property in labor disappear from legal argument. As the connection between rights and property (including property in labor) became more tenuous, the conditions affecting the work of making hats fell outside the sphere of the courts.[18] As a result, legal

17. For many other examples, see the works cited above, n. 5.

18. Here (at the risk of walking into a minefield) it could be said that the work of Rousseau in particular is in need of reexamination. Arguably the novelty of the *Social Contract* lay as much in its attempt to establish a theory of civil rights independent of the natural law concept of property as in any of the more particular concepts that it deployed. It is in general somewhat surprising to find intellectual historians preoccupied with the place of property in modern political theory. Arguably, the distinguishing feature of late eighteenth- and early nineteenth-century theories of society, from Rousseau to Hegel via Adam Smith and Jeremy Bentham, was an attempt to reconcile civil rights with the *absence* of property. This attempt was one of the reasons why a woman like Mary Wollstonecraft could find Rousseau worth taking seriously, whatever he had to say about women in particular. For civil rights for women were the clearest case of the need to find a way of disassociating rights from property.

entitlements of a formal kind acquired the character of informal customs. This essay is a study of that process. At the outset, however, and for much of the eighteenth century, the price of a day's work was also a measure of the various and sometimes disputed rights to which journeymen were entitled.

2

The Ordinary Uses of Hats

Hats themselves were part of the wider context of social meaning and cultural predisposition that informed the public life of eighteenth-century France. Since civil rights were titles of an exceptional kind, they were held to be in the possession of the individuals or collective bodies upon whom they had been conferred. As a result, the line separating the public from the private was not identical to the line separating individuals from the collectivity. An individual was also a public figure, because he (and sometimes she) was, by virtue of occupation or residence or marital status, in possession of certain rights. Public life, in the sense of activities pertaining to public affairs, began at home. This was why hats had a particular significance in the everyday life of eighteenth-century France. They were used to negotiate those occasions on which those endowed with rights of different kinds encountered one another.

Hats, together with swords, pistols, wigs, and stockings, were one of the hallmarks of urban life in eighteenth-century France. The three-cornered hat, worn on the head or carried under the arm, distinguished the inhabitants of towns from those of the country. A model budget drawn up by the silk weavers of Lyon in 1786 included an outlay of 12 livres for a hat that, it was stated, would last for three years.[1] As this provision implies, hats were as much a part of the life of the trades as of high society. The many formal occasions on which artisans participated in the affairs of the collectivity required the use of both a hat and a sword. In 1764 there was

1. Fernand Rude, ed., *Doléances des maîtres-ouvriers, fabricants en étoffes d'or, d'argent, et de soie de la ville de Lyon* (1789; reprint, Lyon, 1976), 20.

an angry meeting of eighty clerks and bookkeepers employed by the leading Parisian hatting firms to oppose a corporate decision denying them the right to carry swords.[2] Hats were less controversial. Until the Revolution and the substitution of the red Phrygian cap for the dark three-cornered hat, the hats that men wore were part of the public life of eighteenth-century France.[3]

Indoors or outdoors, on the head or in the hand, hats were used to orchestrate the conventions of everyday life, transforming suspicion into recognition and real inequality into formal equality. Hats were part of the vocabulary of a silent language employed in the minor dramas of power and submission enacted from day to day. Their presence or absence was apparent only when a cutting phrase or acid observation cast a moment of impropriety into sharp and humiliating relief. Here, for example, is a brief episode, in which a phrase uttered in a few seconds conjures up a world of social nicety. A master locksmith walking past a colleague's workshop in Bordeaux one February day in 1759 was outraged when a journeyman working there called out loudly that his scalp was infected (*qu'il avoit la teigne*). The journeyman later explained that the locksmith was wearing his hat and that it was usual for anyone in the trade who passed a colleague's shop to raise his hat or cap.[4]

Hats, wrote Jean-Baptiste de la Salle in his frequently reprinted *Règles de la bienséance et de la civilité chrétiennes*, should be removed when greeting someone, when in the presence of a social superior, or when offering or receiving a gift. It was,

2. A.N. Y 13 664 (2 December 1764); Y 13 116 (29 December 1764); X[1a] 4488, fol. 373 (19 January 1765); B.N. F 26429. A *commis* employed by Chol et Cie indicated his attitude to the prohibition in a manner that was entirely in keeping with the natural law tradition by stating "qu'il n'est point son ouvrier et que les déffenses . . . ne le regarde pas." A.N. Y 12 166 (10 November 1765).

3. Jennifer Harris, "The Red Cap of Liberty," *Eighteenth-Century Studies* 14 (1981): 283–312.

4. A.D. Gironde, 13B 217 (6 February 1759), interrogation of Laurens Andrieu, who stated "qu'il est d'usage de leur métier de tirer toujours le bonnet ou chapeau quand on passe devant la boutique d'un serrurier."

however, improper to remove one's hat at a formal dinner unless someone worthy of great respect was to arrive. It was improper too to remove one's hat at table if someone of higher rank had done so, for the gesture would be overly familiar. Hats belonged to the ordinary theater of social distinction.[5] The way they were used had elaborate rules. The greatest subtlety was required to extricate oneself—without turning embarrassment into aggression—from a situation in which the rules had been violated. It was right, wrote de la Salle, that a superior should expect an inferior to cover himself after the initial moment of greeting, but it was dangerous to ask him to do so abruptly or tactlessly. To ask someone to cover himself was acceptable only in the presence of an individual of much lower status. It was indecent (*une grande incivilité*) to order a superior to put on his hat. The injunction could be made only to people of equal condition or those with whom one was on familiar terms.[6] The art, of course, was to find ways of violating the rules, to flatter one's interlocutor by creating the fiction of equality.

Hats belonged to public life, and public life included sitting down to dinner, going to the theater, or drinking in a *cabaret*.[7] Public life took place indoors as well as outdoors

5. The subject is discussed by Richard Sennett, *The Fall of Public Man* (London, 1977); see also Pierre Bourdieu, *La Distinction: Critique sociale du jugement* (Paris, 1980). The history of clothing in the eighteenth century is almost nonexistent. See, however, Philippe Perrot, *Les Dessus et les dessous de la bourgeoisie* (Paris, 1981); Paul Lacroix, *XVIIIe Siècle: Institutions, usages, et costumes* (Paris, 1875).

6. Cited in Alfred Franklin, *La Civilité, l'étiquette, la mode: Le Bon Ton aux XVIIIe et XIXe siècles*, 2 vols. (Paris, 1908), 1:138–42. There were, of course, other opinions on the uses to which the *tricorne* in particular was put: "N'étoit-il pas ridicule de l'employer incessamment à la main à des exercices de civilité et de minauderie." Louis Sébastien Mercier, *Tableau de Paris*, 12 vols. (Amsterdam, 1782–88), 4:57–58.

7. For an example of how this distinction between public and private spheres was recognized in a dispute in the hatting trade in Marseille, see below, chapter 10. Mercier's remarks on the three-cornered hat derive from the same assumptions: "C'est toujours celui-là qu'on porte sous le bras lorsqu'on est habillé; mais on ne s'habille plus qu'une ou deux fois la semaine. On voit les gens comme il faut, à l'heure même du spectacle, le chapeau sur la tête." *Tableau de Paris* 4:60.

and possession of a hat was an acknowledgment of the codes that governed admission to the particular sphere of public life in question. Not surprisingly, fights among journeymen (which frequently originated in disputed claims to publicly sanctioned rights to particular kinds of work) often ended triumphantly, if provisionally, in the capture of an opponent's hat. A journeyman joiner arrested in Bordeaux in 1787 for assaulting another journeyman accused the plaintiff of having him arrested to avoid having to pay off his debts. His victim replied, with all the self-righteousness of a person for whom justice has at last been done, that he was having him arrested for assault and that the proof of the assault was the hat he owned, which his assailant was wearing on his head.[8]

Hats bearing the distinctively colored ribbons that were the hallmarks of the associations of itinerant journeymen known as the *compagnonnages* were particularly prized. A crowd of over forty journeymen stonecutters (*tailleurs de pierre*) gathered menacingly outside a joiner's workshop in Bordeaux early in 1776 to reclaim such a hat, which had been captured in a fight. They warned that unless the hat was returned by four o'clock that afternoon there would be trouble in every joiners' shop.[9]

8. "Ah, Ah, tu me fais arrêter pour avoir payé tes dettes," the defendant said. "Non," said the other, "c'est parce que tu m'as maltraité. Tu ne te rappelle pas que vous étiez une douzaine contre moy et que tu étais du nombre." "Je ne t'ai point battu," denied the arrested man. "La preuve que tu m'as battu," came the reply, "c'est qu'il me fut enlevé un chapeau lorsque tu me battais, et ce chapeau tu l'as sur la tête." A.D. Gironde, 12B 382 (31 December 1787), deposition of Jean Delfau. For other examples see ibid., 12B 318 (15 May 1761), deposition of François Hameau; 12B 333 (1 February 1768), deposition of Jean Rambaud; 12B 355 (27 August 1776); 12B 376 (7 April 1785), deposition of Jean Vantage.

9. "Si nous n'avons ce chapeau cette apres-midy à quatre heures nous irons chez tous les menuisiers et nous verrons beau jeu," they warned. Ibid., 12B 354 (5 January 1776), deposition of Jean Baptiste Bordes. A surviving "Livre des compagnon serruries [sic] de la ville et faubourg de Bordeaux" confiscated by the police authorities in 1758 contains a rubric recording fines of 10 sous for "chapeaux perdus" by members of the rite. Eleven contraventions were listed for a six-month period in 1758 (A.D. Gironde, C 3708, fol. 39).

Hats evoked hierarchy and precedence. In the trades, they symbolized the authority of master artisans. They were also symbols of journeymen's ambiguous attitudes toward that authority. During a period of hostility between masters and journeymen in the Parisian bakery trade in the early 1760s, a journeyman warned a master baker to look to himself and his affairs. The journeymen had had his hat during the past year, he said, and now they wanted his wig.[10] There were also, of course, hierarchies among journeymen. A journeyman carpenter from Lyon complained how, on a trade holiday in 1764, he had been out walking in the Croix-Rousse with others in the trade and, to amuse themselves, they had formed their hats into a pile to play a game of leapfrog. The game degenerated into a brawl when one of their leaders insisted that he was entitled to jump first.[11]

Acts like these and the attitudes upon which they were based have an alien and unfamiliar appearance. The aim of this study is to show how the intricacies of everyday life revealed by such incidents also informed the ways in which hats were made. For both the courtesies of daily life and the modalities of making hats were informed by—and underpinned—a wider political culture. In the course of the eighteenth century, the conceptual foundations of that culture began to disintegrate. The particular vantage point of an eighteenth-century trade is an opportunity to explore its premises and logic in concrete and practical terms. It is a culture that is now almost entirely forgotten or, when recalled, placed under the misleading rubric of "popular culture." Journeymen in the hatting trade did not, however, inhabit a cultural netherworld divorced from the conven-

---

10. "Comme ils avaient eu son chapeau l'année passée, ils voulaient avoir sa perruque." A.N. Y 14 091 (1 March 1764). For other examples in eighteenth-century Paris, see ibid., Y 11 239 (15 September 1752); Y 15 350 (17 June 1752, 19 October 1752); Y 14 436 (19 January 1788); Y 15 117 (9 June 1788).

11. "Un des chefs desdits compagnons, et qui en cette qualité prétendoit avoir le pas avant le plaignant et sauter avant luy." A.D. Rhône, BP 3304 (24 July 1764).

tions of public life. In this, their attitudes and behavior were typical of journeymen in many of the urban trades of eighteenth-century France.[12]

Journeymen in the hatting trade made two hats a day even when prevailing techniques and their own circumstances implied that they could have made more. The reasons why they did so lie outside the details of productive processes themselves. What happened when hats were made was, in microcosm, what happened when eighteenth-century French society went about its ordinary affairs. The meaning of the work echoed the wider codes of social life. Just as the places where hats were worn and the uses to which they were put disclose assumptions about the relationship between the public and the private that are recognizably alien, so the procedures informing how hats were made disclose assumptions about the meaning of work that also require elucidation.

12. The question is discussed more extensively in Sonenscher, *Work and Wages.*

3

Customs and Conflict

Artisanal production is invested with an aura of stability, continuity, and an abiding concern with the precepts of custom. Its history often takes the form of an opposition between gemeinschaft and gesellschaft: between the customary norms and moral communities of preindustrial societies and the market values and competitive individualism of industrial societies.[1] That opposition is grounded upon many of the apparently distinctive features of the culture of artisans: its concern with traditional rights, its interest in the maintenance of established skills, its preoccupation with the past, and its emphasis upon the particularity of specific trades.

Yet the antithesis between moral communities and competitive individualism begs as many questions as it appears to answer. For many of the apparently distinctive features of artisanal culture derived from forms of legal argument that were not confined to the trades. Artisans in eighteenth-century France did not simply invent rights or claim obligations. They made use of the courts to place their own

1. I have taken these phrases from Berg, *The Age of Manufactures,* 159, only because the book happened to be at hand. Thus: "The skilled workers of the artisan trades . . . regarded their skilled trades as 'moral communities' in which their art was a source of honour. Journeymen fought their masters in the eighteenth and early nineteenth centuries to prevent the breakdown of their moral communities before the onset of competitive individualism." For some second thoughts, see Jacques Rancière, "The Myth of the Artisan: Critical Reflections on a Category of Social History," in Kaplan and Koepp, *Work in France,* 317–34. More generally, on the limitations of the notions of "popular culture" and "moral communities," see Roger Chartier, "Culture as Appropriation: Popular Cultural Uses in Early Modern Europe," in Steven L. Kaplan, ed., *Understanding Popular Culture* (Berlin, 1984), 229–53, and Giovanni Levi, "I Pericoli del Geertzismo," *Quaderni Storici* 58 (1985): 269–77.

inflections upon forms of legal entitlement embedded within the conventions of natural law. Here, the rights and needs of the producer were given a particular emphasis. For civil rights were titles of a limited kind, whose possession embodied the particular needs and concerns of those upon whom they had been conferred. In the course of the eighteenth century, however, the rights and needs of society as a whole acquired a more positive place in civil jurisprudence. As they did so, rights became customs.

Customs themselves also have a misleading appearance of continuity and stability. In 1885 workers employed on the finishing side of the Parisian hatting trade recorded their determination to adhere to a system of payment by the piece. The system was, they stated, the one best suited to their way of life and independence.[2] Yet throughout the eighteenth century their counterparts had always been paid by the day and had been prepared to go to considerable lengths to maintain a system that they felt was best suited to *their* way of life and independence. Customs are not static and memory is often selective.

Yet the image of custom as, in some way, immune to market imperatives remains. Another episode from outside the period of this study appears to sanction the image. In October 1817 the mayor of Lyon issued a *tarif,* or graduated scale of piece rates, that was designed to bring the level of wages paid to workers in the hatting trade into line with those paid in towns and villages outside the city. The difference in wage levels, the ruling stated, was the result of a series of restrictive practices observed by workers in the hatting trade of Lyon. A certain number of the firms where they worked were known as *fabriques en règle.* The rule in question consisted of limiting output to no more than two hats a day.[3]

2. "Le travail aux pièces est le plus approprié à nos moeurs et à notre indépendance." *L'Ouvrier chapelier* (15 February 1885), cited in Jean Vial, *La Coutume chapelière: Histoire du mouvement ouvrier dans la chapellerie* (Paris, 1941), 115.

3. The practice "provient de l'abus introduit par les ouvriers chapeliers de Lyon de limiter le travail dans les ateliers de la ville, tandis que dans les

The workers responsible for the practice were known as *fouleurs*, or felters. As the name implies, their work consisted of transforming fur into malleable felt. The restrictive practice was an old one. Yet it too was not immutable. The work of making hats changed and so too did the content of certain customary practices. Thus, before returning to the question of how many hats were made in a day, a brief outline of the work of making hats is indispensable. The hatting trade, like most others, was made up of a relatively elaborate division of labor. Unlike most others, however (the work of making a coach or even a piece of fabric, for example), that division of labor was relatively highly integrated. Making a hat in eighteenth-century France involved some three dozen separate processes carried out by at least five different groups of workers, all working in the same place.[4] Figures 1–5, from Jean Antoine Nollet's *L'Art de faire des chapeaux* (Paris, 1765), illustrate the principal operations.

---

communes environnantes, ainsi que dans quelques fabriques qui ne sont point ce qu'on appelle, par un abus coupable, *fabrique en règle,* où le travail n'est point limité, un ouvrier fait beaucoup plus d'ouvrage qu'à Lyon." Georges Bourgin and Hubert Bourgin, *Les Patrons, les ouvriers, et l'état: Le Régime de l'industrie en France de 1814 à 1830,* 3 vols. (Paris, 1912–41), 1:92. On events in the hatting trade in Lyon at this time, see Antonino De Francesco, *Il sogno della repubblica: Il mondo del lavoro dall'Ancien Régime al 1848* (Milan, 1983), 336–53.

4. Descriptions of the techniques of the trade can be found in Jean Antoine Nollet, *L'Art de faire des chapeaux* (Paris, 1765); Denis Diderot et al., *Encyclopédie* (Paris, 1752), s.v. "Chapelier"; *Encyclopaedia Britannica* (Edinburgh, 1771), vol. 2, s.v. "Hat"; Bibliothèque municipale de Rouen, MS. 884[b], "Mémoire sur la fabrique des chapeaux de Paris" (1733). There are several studies of the hatting trade. Most of them are based on limited documentation and, as a result, have not addressed the questions presented here. The fullest is Antonino De Francesco, "Conflittualità sul lavoro in epoca pre-industriale: Le agitazioni degli operai cappellai lionesi (1770–1824)," *Annali della Fondazione Luigi Einaudi* 13 (1979): 151–213. See too the same author's *Il sogno della repubblica.* Although I have not followed his interpretation of the events in Lyon, I am grateful to Dr. De Francesco for directing me to several documents of whose existence I was unaware. Other studies of the trade are Vial, *La Coutume chapelière;* Joseph Fournier, "Une Grève à Marseille en 1785," *Repertoire des travaux de la Société statistique de Marseille* 45 (1900–1901): 223–27. See also Maurice Garden, *Lyon et les Lyonnais au XVIIIe siècle* (Paris, 1970).

Fig. 1. Tearing and shaving fur from pelts

Fig. 2. Bowing the fur

Fig. 3.   Building a hat

Fig. 4.   Felting a hat

Fig. 5.   Dyeing and finishing hats

The preparatory work of tearing and shaving fur from the pelts (fig. 1) was done by women called *coupeuses, arracheuses,* and *repasseuses.* The work was heavily labor-intensive since at least three to four pounds of pelt were needed to produce a pound of fur.[5] It is probable that many of the women who worked in the trade were the wives or daughters of journeymen. This at least was the assumption made by the director of an ephemeral royal manufactory established in Rennes in 1776 in a letter to a Parisian hatter asking him to find two able and skillful *coupeuses.* His preference was for widows or older women who would be unlikely to become pregnant or leave to get married, and whose husbands could be employed if they were skilled in the art of felting fine furs.[6]

5. A.D. Ile-et-Vilaine, C 1509 (13 October 1779).
6. "Nous désirerions bien que ces coupeuses fussent veuves ou d'un âge un peu avancé pour avoir l'espérance de les conserver. S'il se trouvoit qu'elles fussent mariées à de bons fouleurs en fin et que leurs maris voulus-

Once stripped from the pelt the fur was then sorted by color, carded, weighed, and given out in measured amounts to be felted. The work done by felters consisted of two separate processes. The first (fig. 2) involved freeing the fur of dirt and tangles and enhancing its suppleness. This process was performed with a bowing instrument known as an *arçon*, which was passed repeatedly through the piles of fur as the string was made to vibrate. The work was hot and dirty because it required an enclosed, draft-free room. It resulted in the creation of four, six, or eight conically shaped piles of fur called *capades* in France and "bats" in England. These piles were covered with pieces of damp cloth and placed upon one another to form the basis of a hat. The hat was, in this way, "built" from "planks" (fig. 3). The *fouleurs* then carried out the second major process (fig. 4). They took the materials to a trough or round metal basin filled with a mixture of wine waste or sediment (*lie de vin*) and hot water to be fulled or felted.

The felt was then placed on a wooden mold and left to dry. These molds varied in size and were modified as fashions changed, so that a hatting concern could have a large number of them. The enterprise in Rennes, which went bankrupt in 1784, had over six hundred.[7] Even a very tiny workshop like one in the Norman village of Beuzeville-la-Grenier had a dozen.[8]

Once dry, the hats were finished by another group of journeymen, called *approprieurs* and *apprêteurs* (fig. 5). The journeymen singed the hats over a fire, rubbed them with a

---

sent les suivre, nous les recevrons." Ibid., C 1510, Anthéaume to Fauchereaux, rue Galande, Paris (7 December 1777). Nineteen women employed in the trade of Marseille gave evidence in legal proceedings arising from disputes in 1761 and 1774. Eight were single and (apart from two women of thirty-five and thirty-six) were aged under twenty-five; two were widows in their fifties; the rest were married, half of them to men working in the trade (A.C. Marseille, FF 370 and 383).

7. A.D. Ile-et-Vilaine, C 1513.

8. Margueritte Bruneau, "Une Famille de chapeliers à Beuzeville-la-Grenier au XVIIIe siècle," in *Cahiers Leopold Delisle* 32 (1982–83), special issue on "Travail, métiers, et professions en Normandie" (Paris, 1984), 115–24.

pumice stone and sealskin to raise the nap, and trimmed them before they were taken to be dyed. As many as twelve dozen hats could be dyed at once. After the hats had been dyed and allowed to dry, the *apprêteurs* completed the finishing process by steaming each hat over a vat in order to force in a stiffening agent—usually gum arabic or gum senegal—which had been brushed into its surface with great care. This part of the process was the most delicate of operations. As an early eighteenth-century observer wrote, there was no standard procedure, so that much depended upon the ability of the worker.[9] The hats were finally trimmed and tidied by a fifth group of workers—again usually women—known as *éjarreuses*. Subsequently, embellishments of different kinds—feathers, gilt, or silk ribbons—were added. In some cases, this work also took place on the premises. More usually, however, it was done elsewhere. In this respect, the division of labor in the hatting trade was similar to the dis-integrated division of labor found in many other trades.

The *tarif* ratified by the municipal authorities in Lyon in 1817 applied principally to the work done by felters. It caused some raised eyebrows in ministerial circles in Paris. The ruling was, as the minister of the interior observed, incompatible with current legislation and the true principles of political economy.[10] In September 1819, however, he was sent a description of working practices in the hatting trade of Lyon by the local *lieutenant de police* that were themselves not entirely compatible with the principles of political economy. It had been shown, the *lieutenant de police* wrote, that a worker of ordinary ability could make at least three hats a day. But, he continued, workers in Lyon had agreed to make no more than two so that everyone could be employed and the most able did not get all the work themselves.[11]

9. "N'y ayant point de règle certaine pour cette operation, qui réellement est sçavante." B.M. Rouen, MS. 884[b].

10. Bourguin and Bourguin, *Les Patrons* 1:267.

11. "Ces mêmes ouvriers sont convenus entre eux de ne pas faire plus de deux chapeaux chacun par jour, afin que tous soient occupés et que le plus habile n'enlève pas le travail à celui qui l'est moins." Ibid. 1:269–70.

Workshops where this practice was observed were known as *fabriques en règle;* the others were termed *fabriques non en règle.* The former were the largest enterprises and produced the best-quality goods. The latter were smaller and more numerous.[12] Employers in the latter category were more usually found plying their trade in tiny workshops on the upper, cheaper floors of apartment blocks. They were more likely to use stolen materials, producing cheaper goods on the shoddy side of the trade. By contrast, workshops where the rule applied were places where workers enjoyed a substantial degree of autonomy in the workplace. They had an elaborate system of fines, found work for one another, decided how hats should be made, fixed the number they were prepared to make, and refused to work with anyone who had violated their rules.[13]

These practices appear to be a case of a phenomenon that has been widely discussed by historians of early modern European society.[14] Workers were content to earn enough to meet their essential needs and would not do any additional work once this threshold had been reached. The phenomenon has been given the graceless title of a "backward-bending supply curve of labor."

12. "Ils nomment les uns fabriques en règle, et les autres fabriques non en règle. Les fabriques en règle sont les plus importantes pour la fortune des fabricants, le nombre des ouvriers et la qualité des chapeaux. Les fabriques dites non en règle sont en seconde ligne et plus nombreuses." Ibid. 1:270.

13. "Les ouvriers appellent fabriques en règle celles où ils établissent des amendes, placent des compagnons, indiquent la manière dont les chapeaux seront faits, le degré de la perfection de la main d'oeuvre, fixent le nombre de chapeaux auquel doit se borner chaque ouvrier par jour. . . . C'est là, enfin, où les ouvriers imposent des amendes dont ils sont eux-mêmes les arbitres et à défaut desquelles ils interdisent le travail, jusqu'à ce que l'ouvrier ait payé l'amende qui lui a été infligée." Ibid.

14. For a survey and more extensive bibliography, see Peter Mathias, *The Transformation of England* (London, 1979), 148–67. An initial attempt to discuss the question can be found in Michael Sonenscher, "Work and Wages in Eighteenth-Century Paris," in M. Berg, P. Hudson, and M. Sonenscher, eds., *Manufacture in Town and Country Before the Factory* (London, 1983). A fuller, and slightly different, presentation will be found in Sonenscher, *Work and Wages.*

The report on working practices in the hatting trade of Lyon in 1819 appears to confirm that the phenomenon existed. Workers limited the amount of time they spent at work not only because they were able to earn enough in four days rather than six but because the practice ensured that more people would be able to find work in the trade than would otherwise have been possible. The phenomenon was apparently limited, however, to the largest and most prosperous hatting concerns. It appears to be one of those anonymous and timeless customary norms that were traditional to the trades of early modern Europe.

In this instance, however, it is possible to give this customary norm a history. As a result, it is possible to divest the practices of a trade of their anonymous and timeless appearance and establish links between them and the wider political culture. For the norm in question was relatively recent in origin. Fifty years previously, in 1773, manufacturers in the hatting trade in Lyon also drew the attention of the authorities to the working practices of journeymen. At that time, however, they recorded that felters were not prepared to make more than nine hats a week.[15] Traditional practices were capable apparently of accommodating considerable increases in productivity. Between 1773 and 1819 the customary norm recognized on the felting side of the trade rose by a third. On the finishing side too what was customary was not necessarily what had always been observed. As has been mentioned, workers on the finishing side of the trade in late nineteenth-century Paris insisted upon their customary right to payment by the piece, although they had been paid by the day a hundred years previously.

The emergence of these ambiguous traditions was the product of a series of changes that occurred in the hatting trade during the latter half of the eighteenth century. These changes were not confined to the city of Lyon but took place

15. A.C. Lyon, HH 32, "Mémoire des maîtres chapeliers de Lyon" (September 1773). On the events that gave rise to this observation, see below, chapter 9.

concurrently in the two other major centers of the hatting trade, Paris and Marseille. Nor were they limited to the felting side of the trade. They affected the whole range of the various phases of production and intruded into the wider environment of productive relations. They came to be symbolized by one particular technical innovation. This was the practice of adding mercury to a solution used to treat pelts from which fur used to make hats was taken. The practice was revealed to the wider public domain in the last decade of the Old Regime. In the spring of 1784, the Académie royale des sciences of Paris announced a competition to determine the nature and causes of the illnesses suffered by workers employed in the manufacture of hats.[16] Eighteen months later, in October 1785, the chemist and philosophe Antoine-Laurent Lavoisier recommended the award of the prize to an essay by a Genevan doctor named Gosse—appropriately bearing an epigraph familiar to admirers of Rousseau: "Love of man, derived from the love of oneself, is the very principle of justice."[17]

At first sight the epigraph seems somewhat misplaced in a medical treatise devoted to the microscopic analysis of the fibrous structure of fur. Its meaning is more evident in the light of events in the hatting trade at the time. Between 1784 and 1786 journeymen in Paris, Lyon, and Marseille were also preoccupied with the principle of justice. At least three separate but related court cases, punctuated by a series of stoppages, were indicative of their concerns. The two events—the competition and the litigation—were not unrelated. They form a moment at which it is possible to identify two different ways of ascribing meanings to the work which people did. In one mode work was invested with a language that emphasized its

16. A. L. Lavoisier, *Oeuvres* (Paris, 1893), 6:12–15.

17. Bibliothèque publique et universitaire de Genève, Manuscrit français 1681, Henri-Albert Gosse, "Mémoire en réponse à une question posée par l'Académie des sciences de Paris en 1784," fol. 1. My translation is a feeble attempt to capture some of the force of an aphorism—"L'amour des hommes, dérivé de l'amour de soi-même, est le principe de la justice lui-même"—whose sense owes everything to Rousseau's distinction between *amour propre* and *amour de soi*.

importance as "one of the sources of the prosperity of estates, satisfying our needs and increasing our pleasures in a thousand different ways."[18] In another it was endowed with a language of rights and obligations that made little reference to the possible benefits of what was produced but referred, instead, almost exclusively to the condition and status of the producer.

Changes in the internal life of the hatting trade during the second half of the eighteenth century resulted in the emergence of a clear distinction between these two modes. The difference between work as social production (and, as such, invested with the general rights and obligations of society) and work as productive capacity (and, as such, invested with the particular rights and obligations of the producer) was central to the question of the number of hats that could be made in a day. The events that took place in Paris, Lyon, and Marseille between 1784 and 1786 captured the tension in that difference in the history of a single trade.

That history unfolded in a sequence of disputes that began during the Seven Years' War and continued intermittently until the Revolution (fig. 6). The word "sequence" is used deliberately. A series of conflicts in several different localities over a period of more than a generation would not normally be treated as a unity. Although particular circumstances were often the occasion for disputes in the hatting trade, there were also continuities of attitudes, practices, and personnel from one episode to the next that transcended the immediate context in which conflict occurred. Each episode was informed by the participants' awareness of previous disputes and the outcome of different events in other localities. The whole sequence discloses a continuum of attitudes and actions whose internal coherence is indicative of the broader, and still largely unknown, cultural world of eighteenth-century French artisans.

18. "Une des sources de la prospérité des états, pourvoyant à nos besoins, multipliant de mille manières nos jouissances." Gosse, "Mémoire," fol. 1.

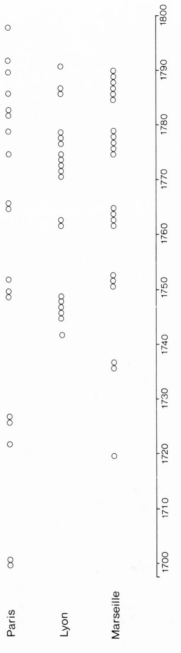

Fig. 6. Disputes in the hatting trade in the eighteenth century

○ = A year in which a dispute occurred or was in progress

To enter this cultural world, it is necessary to abandon the parochialism that has informed the study of artisans in eighteenth-century France. This is a study of a trade in a number of different localities, some very distant from one another. Yet both the structure of the trade and the preoccupations of those whose livelihoods depended upon it make it difficult to understand its history within the context of a single town or city. In this the hatting trade may have been exceptional. It is also possible, however, that studies of artisans limited to the analysis of marriage contracts, the contents of inventories, the presence or absence of signatures on parish registers, or attitudes toward death disclosed by the terms of wills have divested the history of the urban trades—and much of eighteenth-century French urban society as well—of more than a little of their social and cultural substance. To recover that substance it is necessary to go beyond the particularism induced by too close a dependence upon parish registers and notarial records (without, it should be emphasized, discarding what they reveal) and turn to three broader areas. The first is the organization of the hatting trade itself. The second is the relationship between the law and the work that hatters did. The third is the identity of journeymen's association in the trade. Together they supply the context informing the disputed question of the number of hats it was possible to make in a day. As they changed, so the significance of the work itself changed, and the tension between the image of production as the satisfaction of social needs and the image of the producer as an individual endowed with certain distinctive rights became increasingly clear.

4

The Division of Labor

Throughout the eighteenth century the fortunes of the hatting trade in France were tied to those of the trading diasporas that were its main source of primary materials and its major non-domestic market.[1] In this respect, the trade had more in common with the production of high-quality textiles like silks or textiles like calicoes that were dependent upon non-European sources of dyestuffs than it had with urban trades that could draw upon more varied sources of supply and final markets. Furs imported from North America or Russia were the trade's staple primary material. Fur had been used to make hats for many hundreds of years. Any fur could be used: in his prizewinning essay Gosse examined the possibility of making hats from the fur of camels, llamas, spaniels, and moles, as well as the more usual rabbits, hares, vicuñas, marten, lynx, or the wool of sheep. The fur that was most celebrated during the seventeenth and eighteenth centuries and was used to produce the finest quality hats was, however, that of the beaver.

Beaver hats were made for the more prosperous inhabitants of the towns. The three-cornered hat (*tricorne*) is a familiar component of eighteenth-century depictions of public life, owned by journeymen and master artisans as well as professional and military men. Many of these hats were, however, made from wool or rabbit fur. Hats made from

1. The term "trading diaspora" is borrowed from Philip D. Curtin, *Cross-Cultural Trade in World History* (London, 1984); on the North-American fur trade, see Harold A. Innis, *The Fur Trade in Canada* (Toronto, 1956); Daniel Francis and Toby Morantz, *Partners in Furs* (Kingston and Montreal, 1983); W. J. A. Eccles, "A Belated Review of Harold Adams Innes, *The Fur Trade in Canada*," *Canadian Historical Review* 40 (1979): 420–41.

beaver were stronger, finer, and considerably more expensive. In 1782 a hatter in the small *cévenol* town of Anduze advertised ordinary men's hats for between 3 and 6 livres. Beaver hats were priced at between 12 and 24 livres.[2] Thus although the hatting trade could be found in almost every eighteenth-century French town, so that even relatively tiny localities like Cholet, Niort, Uzès, or Evreux as well as many villages had two or three hatters, the production of beaver hats was confined essentially to Rouen (in the early eighteenth century), Paris, Lyon, and Marseille.

The large merchant-manufacturing concerns of the three cities supplied beaver hats to an essentially urban, artisanal, and rentier-aristocratic clientele through a variety of intermediaries and retailers. Throughout the eighteenth century, the retail side of the trade depended upon the great fairs of Beaucaire, Guibray, Caen, and Bordeaux for a proportion of its wholesale supplies.[3] There were also military and naval contracts to be found, for army officers above the rank of sergeant also wore beaver hats, while ordinary foot soldiers, cavalrymen, and dragoons wore woolen hats.[4] Sales in France were complemented by markets beyond the frontiers: in Italy, Spain, Portugal, the French colonies in the Caribbean, and the Spanish settlements in South America.[5] There, competition with the English hatting trade was an abiding concern to manufacturers, especially in Lyon and Marseille. Figures for

2. A.D. Gard 1 Mi. 90, papers of the partnership of Rose, Pelatan et Cie of Anduze; B.H.V.P. MS. CP 4858.

3. On the fairs of Beaucaire, Guibray, and Caen, see Pierre Léon, "Vie et mort d'un grand marché international: La Foire de Beaucaire," *Revue de géographie de Lyon* 28 (1953): 309–28; and Jean-Claude Perrot, *Genèse d'une ville moderne: Caen au XVIIIe siècle*, 2 vols. (Paris, 1975), 1:467–94, 2:738–42.

4. A.D. Ile-et-Vilaine, C 1508, *arrêt du Conseil* (26 January 1746), defining the types of hats to be used by the troops.

5. The Spanish embargo upon imports of manufactured goods from France in 1778 affected the hatting trade as well as the hosiery trade and produced a coordinated campaign by the hatters of Paris, Lyon, and Marseille to have it revoked. See A.D. Bouches-du-Rhône, 367E^{265}, fol. 954 (7 November 1775); 367E^{270}, fol. 63 (4 January 1779); 367E^{275}, fol. 338 (28 February 1783); and Archives de la Chambre de Commerce de Lyon, Missives (1740–81) fol. 214v (28 October 1775).

the size of the export market do not exist, but the insistence with which hatters in Lyon and Marseille, particularly after 1730, emphasized the importance of markets in southern Europe and the need to match the quality and prices of English hats is an indication of the strategic significance of international markets both for marginal profits and as a source of pressure upon costs.[6] In this respect, the hatting trade had many similarities to the French hosiery trade, whose principal external markets were also in southern Europe. Hatters in Paris, Lyon, and Marseille, like hosiers in Nîmes and Lyon, protested strongly when the Spanish Crown introduced an embargo upon imported hats and stockings in 1778.[7]

Figures do not exist for either the quantity of hats produced or the size of the trade as a whole, but indirect evidence indicates that the trade was growing in size during the eighteenth century. In Lyon the proportion of hatters among the artisans who signed marriage contracts rose from under 3 percent to over 8 percent between the late 1720s and the late 1780s, and there is no reason to suppose that conditions in Paris or Marseille were any different.[8] The preamble to a ruling by the Royal Council (Conseil d'état) in 1770 announced that the total production of the trade provided a living for over a hundred thousand families, including six thousand in Paris alone.[9] The figure is an exaggerated guess.

---

6. The absence of any records concerning the scale of the export trade makes the identity and size of foreign markets impossible to establish in any precise way. There is no reason to suppose that the French hatting trade differed greatly from its English counterpart, where in 1736 beaver hats accounted for over 80 percent of the value of hat exports (David Corner, "The London Hatting Trade, 1660–1800," unpublished paper presented to the Pasold Conference on the Economic and Social History of Dress [London, September 1985]). Qualitative statements on the importance of southern Europe and success against English competition can be found in A.D. Rhône, 3E 7879 (19 September 1735); 3E 7883 (11 February 1739).

7. See n. 4 above. On the hosiery trade, see Michael Sonenscher, "Royalists and Patriots: Nîmes and Its Sénéchaussée in the Late Eighteenth Century" (Ph.D. thesis, University of Warwick, 1978).

8. Garden, *Lyon et les Lyonnais*, 316.

9. A.D. Ile-et-Vilaine, C 1508, *arrêt du Conseil* (16 September 1770).

A simple multiplication of the number of localities in the late eighteenth century with populations of 2,000 inhabitants or more by a hypothetical average of 5 hatters suggests an order of magnitude of some 3,705 master hatters.[10]

Precision is impossible. The fact that the trade was widely distributed among the towns of eighteenth-century France is, however, of some importance. Much is often made of the skills and esoteric techniques of artisanal production. There is, of course, some truth in the claim—as anyone who has seen a piece of eighteenth-century furniture or wrought iron-work will admit. Yet the materials used in most trades in the eighteenth century were relatively widely available, and opportunities to acquire a rudimentary knowledge of the techniques needed to transform them into finished articles were not greatly limited. The elaborate prescriptions of eighteenth-century apprenticeship regulations conceal imperatives that owed as much to formal definitions of adulthood, family strategies, and local economic circumstances as to the techniques of the trades. Once they were abolished the length of an apprenticeship could vary from six months to six years in exactly the same trade.[11] Everything depended upon the age

10. There were 741 *communes* with populations of 2,000 or more inhabitants in the first decade of the nineteenth century (R. Le Mée, "Population agglomérée, population éparse au début du XIXe siècle," *Annales de démographie historique* [1971]: 455–510). The number of journeymen is even more problematic. It is likely that most hatters in little towns like Châteauduloir or Saint-Calais depended almost entirely upon their own families' resources and that large numbers of journeymen were to be found only in the main centers of urban production. The effects of this state of affairs are discussed in chapter 5.

11. A.C. Anduze (Gard), FF 23, register of *livrets* issued by the municipality, 1803–20. The register records the lengths of apprenticeships served by journeymen to whom *livrets* were issued. From this record, it is clear that there was an inverse relationship between the length of an apprenticeship and the age at which it was begun. A boy of twelve or thirteen would serve an apprenticeship of five or six years; someone of sixteen or seventeen would serve a much shorter time. These remarks run counter to recent discussions of the notion of skill and especially to the assumption that capitalist development and "de-skilling" are related. Some thoughts on the question can be found in Michael Sonenscher, "The Meaning of Skill in Eighteenth-Century France" (unpublished paper presented to the Workshop on Social Practices, European University Institute, Florence, 1984).

of a boy when the apprenticeship began. In many respects skill—in the sense of limited access to specialized and esoteric techniques—is a more modern phenomenon than has been assumed. In the eighteenth-century French trades wood, leather, and the ordinary wool used in making hats in many localities were relatively easily available. Skill was therefore relatively widely disseminated and, in anything other than the very short term, labor was in relatively abundant supply. In the hatting trade skill enjoyed a fragile association with certain materials, and with beaver fur in particular.

Familiarity with beaver fur was what distinguished the journeymen who worked in Paris, Lyon, and Marseille from their thousands of counterparts in cities like Amiens, Reims, Tours, or Montpellier. It was particularly necessary on the felting side of the trade, where a journeyman's ability consisted of knowing how long to press and roll the felt so that it reached the highest level of consistency. According to the master hatters of Lyon in 1735, six or seven hours were needed to produce the felt for a fine hat, although hats made of inferior materials could withstand no more than three hours of fulling.[12] As a result, journeymen from Paris, Lyon, or Marseille (and the first two cities in particular) were highly prized. Production of beaver hats elsewhere in France depended heavily upon the technical competence of hatters from one or another of the three major cities. The ephemeral *manufacture royale* established in Rennes in 1776 relied upon the experience of a former Parisian master hatter. A pair of enterprises established in Givors and Anduze were set up by hatters from Lyon.[13]

The manufactory in Rennes measured the quality of its output against the standards set by the firms of Veuve

12. "Il faitte [sic] ordinairement employer six à sept heures à cette opération pour toutes sortes de bons chapeaux." A.D. Rhône, 3E 7879 (19 September 1735).

13. In each case involving imitations of English techniques (see A.N. F¹² 558; A.D. Rhône, 3E 9706 [7 February 1764]; and A.D. Gard, 1 Mi. 90). The manufactory at Rennes was created by a Parisian hatter named Anthéaume (see A.N. F¹² 652).

Châtelain et Cie and Chol et Cie, reputedly the two best houses in Paris on the eve of the American War. It emphasized that the quality of its own hats reflected the origins of its felters and finishers in Paris and Lyon.[14] When a commercial house in Nantes complained that the hats produced in Rennes for the Spanish market were inferior to those of Paris and Lyon, its director drafted a vigorous and revealing reply. All his workers, he insisted, had worked in the best houses in Paris and Lyon and would never lose the abilities that they had acquired. It was possible, he agreed, that they had lost something of their touch by working on lower-quality materials in small provincial towns, but the principles informing the production of the best hats could never be lost.[15]

Beaver fur came in two kinds. The English terms "coat beaver" and "parchment beaver" are more expressive of the difference between them than the French terms *castor gras* and *castor sec*. Coat beaver was the fur left on beaver pelts after they had been scraped, greased, and worn as coats by North American Indian trappers before they were exchanged at trading posts in Canada. Worn in this way, the stiff outer guard hairs of the pelt dropped off, leaving the softer, velvety duvet used in the making of hats. Parchment beaver, as its name suggests, was fur from pelts that had not been worn but had been left to dry in the sun before they were traded.

The use of beaver fur in the making of hats was first mentioned in the statutes of the Parisian corporation of hat-

14. "Nous avons un excellent approprieur qui nous est arrivé de Paris il y a un mois et qui sortoit de chez Mme Châtelain, et hier un compagnon fouleur qui sort de chez M. Chol la seconde maison en chapellerie de cette ville." A.D. Ile-et-Vilaine, C 1510, Anthéaume to Morin and Vallin, Nantes (27 March 1778).

15. "Croyent ils," he explained, "que l'artiste et l'ouvrier une fois hors de ces villes perdent leurs talents. . . . Comme je le dis, de bons ouvriers ayant travaillé avec satisfaction dans les ouvrages les plus distingués à Paris et Lyon doivent avoir pour le reste de leurs jours les principes et la manoeuvre d'une bonne fabrication. Je conviens que, fabriquants en province des feutres grossiers il leur faut un peu de tems pour que la main se remette. Mais les principes ne se perdent jamais." Ibid.

makers of 1612.[16] During the second half of the seventeenth century, a series of regulations were introduced to establish a clear distinction between hats made of different types of fur. Formally, until the end of the seventeenth century, hats made of beaver could contain no other fur. The production of woolen hats with a beaver covering, optimistically named *demi-castors*, or half-beavers, was prohibited under the revised statutes of the Parisian corporation of 1658. In 1666 and 1667 the Royal Council ruled that hats described as beaver hats should contain nothing but beaver fur. A further ruling in 1673 again prohibited the production of half-beaver hats. The mercantilist objectives of these regulations were clear. They were designed to establish a durable symmetry between materials, manufactured goods, and markets, so that if the quality of the first of these variables was maintained, control of the other two would follow. A ruling by the council in October 1699, during a glut of unused coat beaver, limited production to two kinds: pure beaver hats and woolen hats made from vicuña and camel fur, "without any rabbit, hare, otter, or any similar kind of fur."[17] This rigid distinction was relaxed a year later, in August 1700, by an *arrêt* ruling that four kinds of hat were acceptable: pure beaver, half-beaver, assorted fur, and wool. Although this ruling was very much more accommodating, it continued to stipulate clearly that the use of hare "and other defective materials" was prohibited.

The *arrêt* of August 1700, the last major intervention by the royal government into the hatting trade, set the broad outlines of legal provisions for the trade in the eighteenth century. Permission to produce half-beaver hats was reiterated in another *arrêt du Conseil* in 1734, which maintained the established sense of the law. The clear distinction between hats made of beaver fur and hats made from the fur of other ani-

16. Alfred Franklin, *Dictionnaire historique des arts, métiers et professions exercés dans Paris depuis le treizième siècle* (Paris, 1906), 140–42. The texts of the rulings referred to can be found in René de Lespinasse, *Les Métiers et corporations de la ville de Paris* (Paris, 1897), 3:272–95.
17. Lespinasse, *Métiers*, 3:272.

mals continued to prevail. Although hats made from the fur of camels, rabbits, vicuñas, and marten were acceptable and the production of *demi-castors* reluctantly permitted, the use of hare in the hatting trade remained entirely prohibited.

The reasons for these distinctions were both fiscal and commercial. The traffic in beaver pelts from North America was a source of royal revenue. Duties on pelts were farmed out to the financiers responsible for the *domaine d'occident* (the tax farm concerned principally with the collection of duties from the colonial trade) and, after 1700, to the ephemeral Compagnie du Canada or Compagnie du castor. This company was one of the less successful trading cum revenue-collecting ventures established during the period of financial improvisation and experiment surrounding the War of the Spanish Succession. By 1705 it was substantially in arrears and was finally absorbed into Law's Compagnie des Indes in 1718.[18]

Revenue from imported pelts was complemented by revenue from duties on manufactured goods. In 1664 a duty was levied upon hats exported to provinces outside the *cinq grosses fermes*, the area covered by the Royal Tax Farmers, and it was logical to expect that the returns from the tax would be the greater if hatters were required to use beaver fur.[19] The injunction to use beaver also had its origins, however, in the need to maintain the quality of the product itself. Hats made from beaver—particularly coat beaver—felted more readily; when properly finished they were firmer, more lustrous, and more durable than hats made from other materials. The quality of the fur in general and of coat beaver in particular was an important element in capturing and retaining markets—especially southern European markets—from English, Dutch, and, later, Spanish competition. The royal administration and the hatters' corporations were in agreement about matters of quality. On a number of

18. Charles W. Cole, *French Mercantilism, 1683–1700* (New York, 1943), 66–77; Thomas J. Schaeper, *The French Council of Commerce, 1700–1715* (Columbus, Ohio, 1983), 242–43.

19. A.N. AD+ 1054 (12 December 1781) for legislation concerning these duties. See also A.N. AB XIX 656 bis.

occasions during the early eighteenth century, the initiative to enforce or clarify regulations governing the content of hats came from the corporations themselves rather than the royal administration.[20]

In the latter half of the seventeenth century, the main manufacturing centers were situated at the two ends of the trading network involved in the supply of materials and the distribution of finished goods: along the Atlantic coast of France, where beaver pelts arrived from North America, Russia, or Amsterdam, and in Lyon and Marseille, the main channels through which goods destined for southern European and Spanish American markets passed. During the period of the wars of the League of Augsburg and the Spanish Succession, the centers of production along the Atlantic coast appear to have lost their importance to the advantage of Paris, Lyon, and—after the devastation of the plague of 1720 had passed—Marseille. Although attempts were made during the eighteenth century to establish manufactories in Rennes, Givors, La Charité-sur-Loire, and Anduze, the production of beaver hats for sale in distant markets continued to distinguish the trades of the three cities of Paris, Lyon, and Marseille from those of other localities.

One reason for this geographical concentration was the role played by the Compagnie des Indes in the supply of beaver pelts from Canada. After the collapse of the Compagnie du Canada in the last years of the reign of Louis XIV, the Compagnie des Indes acquired exclusive control over the trade in beaver pelts from North America in 1718.[21] The close links between the trading company and its Parisian financiers created a highly centralized system of distribution. Although beaver pelts were also imported from Russia and Scandinavia, usually via Amsterdam, the company had effective control over supplies of the all-important coat beaver until the end of the Seven Years' War. The pelts, usually together with

20. See below, chapter 6.
21. A.N. AB XIX 656 bis, "Recueil de règlements sur le commerce des castors"; see also the works referred to in n. 18 above.

Table 1   Distribution of Employment in
the Hatting Trade of Rouen, 1752

Number of Masters	Number of Journeymen Employed
3	0
10	1–5
1	6–10
3	11–20
1	21+
Total 18	100

Source: A.D. Seine-Maritime, 5E 205.

rather larger quantities of parchment beaver, were shipped
to La Rochelle and sent from there to the company's ware-
houses in the capital. Parisian hatters were therefore best
placed to acquire stocks of *castor gras* and *castor sec* from the
company.

It is probable that this advantageous position resulted in
the concentration of the production of *castors* in Paris and
the relative eclipse of the previously substantial hatting
trades of Rouen and Caudebec. Caudebec hats were made
mainly from wool and, by the second quarter of the eighteenth century, were no longer produced for distant markets.[22] The number of master hatters in Rouen fell substantially during the eighteenth century, from between sixty
and seventy-five between 1728 and 1739 to under forty between 1751 and 1783.[23] Only a minority of them actually
manufactured hats, and then on a relatively small scale. In
January 1752, for example, eighteen manufacturers employed a total of one hundred journeymen—a figure that
obviously does not include the women who also worked in
the trade (table 1). Only four hatters employed more than

22. "Les chapeaux de toutes sortes qui se fabriquoient autrefois en
grand nombre dans plusieurs lieux de la généralité [de Rouen], et qui
s'envoyoient en Angleterre, en Hollande et en Allemagne sont presque
réduits à la seule consommation de la province." Savary des Bruslons,
Dictionnaire universel de commerce (1750; reprint, Copenhagen, 1765), 5:177.
23. A.D. Seine-Maritime, 5E 204, 207, 208, 211.

ten journeymen; the largest had ten felters, nine finishers and two dyers working for him. In this respect, the hatting trade of Rouen had come to resemble that of scores of eighteenth-century French towns from Tours to Montpellier and from Toulouse to Reims. In these localities most hatters were retailers or, at most, wholesalers rather than manufacturers; where they did make (or more usually repair) hats, they produced commodities from domestic wools or furs for local or regional consumption. The hatting trades of Paris, Lyon, and Marseille, however, were organized on an altogether different scale.

5

Workshop Size,
the Structure of the Trade, and
the Composition of the Workforce

The trades of Paris, Lyon, and Marseille were substantially larger than those of any other French town. They were integrated into commercial circuits of national or international dimensions for both the supply of their raw materials and their final markets.[1] Entry into the manufacturing side of the trade thus implied relatively substantial resources of capital and credit as well as regular access to considerable amounts of cash to pay the wages of the large number of men and women employed by a single *fabricant*. As a result, only a minority of master hatters ever made hats. The proportion of about one manufacturer to four retailers or repairers in Rouen was probably fairly usual throughout the trade. In Paris there were said to be about three hundred master hatters in 1733, of whom only sixty were engaged in production, including ten who specialized in dyeing hats.[2] A cen-

---

1. By way of comparison there were only a dozen master hatters in Toulouse in the mid-eighteenth century (A.D. Haute-Garonne E 1261) and seventeen in Nîmes in 1769 (A.N. F¹² 780). The hatting trade of Nantes was also composed of retailers and manufacturers of woolen, rather than beaver, hats. In a lawsuit with the local hosiers over their claim to a monopoly of the sale of hats, the hosiers observed that "si les chapeliers établis à Nantes . . . faisoient des chapeaux aussy beaux et au même prix que les chapeaux de Lyon, de Paris, etc., voudroient-ils avoir pour seuls vendeurs les fabricants des autres pays." A.D. Ile-et-Vilaine, 1Bm 241² (1763). In producing for international markets, the hatting trade increasingly came to share some of the features of proto-industries (see P. Kriedte, H. Medick, and J. Schlumbohm, *Industrialization Before Industrialization* (London, 1982); M. Berg et al., eds., *Manufacture in Town and Country Before the Factory* (London, 1983).

2. B.M. Rouen, MS. 884ᵇ.

sus of the labor force made to facilitate the distribution of beaver pelts during a period of acute shortage in 1739 lists 63 manufacturers employing a total of 546 journeymen.[3]

The enumeration also discloses a sharp contrast between large and small enterprises. While the majority of masters (45, or 71 percent) employed less than ten journeymen each, half of the total workforce (272, or 49.8 percent) worked for ten individuals (or 15.9 percent of the total number of masters) employing twenty or more *compagnons* (table 2). Thus, like most eighteenth-century French trades, the hatting trade consisted of a relatively small central core of large establishments where the majority (or a large minority) of journeymen worked and a larger periphery made up of many smaller enterprises in which a relatively small proportion of the workforce was employed.[4]

This bipartite structure was by no means confined to the hatting trade. It is probable, however, that the division between the core and periphery was more rigid in the main centers of large-scale hat production than it was in the majority of the urban trades. A large workforce—and while half a dozen journeymen was a large workforce in the tailoring trade, the number was nearer two dozen in the hatting trade—involved recurrent and relatively substantial wage-costs. In addition, the need for several rooms to prepare and finish materials, the costs of the materials themselves, and the long credit involved in international commerce all served to raise the threshold of entry into the core of the trade.

The implications of this division and of its enduring character were substantial. It meant that entry into the manufacturing side of the trade called for relatively substantial funds, so that its capital requirements had more in common with the textile trades than with most other urban trades. It also meant that a majority of journeymen worked in *fabriques*

3. Bibliothèque de l'Arsenal, MS. Bastille 10321, "Etat de la communauté des chapeliers" (1739).

4. A full discussion of this structure can be found in Sonenscher, *Work and Wages*. There is a large literature on dualism in modern labor markets. See the discussion and works cited in Charles Sabel, *Work and Politics* (London, 1982), 31–77.

Table 2   Distribution of Employment by Workshop Size
in the Parisian Hatting Trade, 1739

Workers per Shop	Masters	Journeymen
1–4	33	86
5–9	12	80
10–19	8	108
20–39	8	184
40+	2	88
Total	63	546

Source: Bibliothèque de l'Arsenal, MS. Bastille 10321.

employing at least twenty other men and women. Labor markets were therefore relatively highly centralized. Conditions of employment in the trade were therefore determined by what happened in a relatively small number of large hatting enterprises. As a result, many apparently local and isolated disputes involving only a tiny proportion of the total number of master hatters in one or other of the three cities often had a much wider significance.

The structure of the trade also ensured that large-scale production was irretrievably out of the range of the great majority of journeymen. Although it was somewhat easier to become a master in the peripheral zone, no journeyman (or only a very few) could meet the formal requirements of admission to a corporation and produce hats on the scale of the small number of enterprises at the core of the principal centers of production. This state of affairs was reflected in the very high price of entry into the hatters' corporations of the three cities. In Paris the price of a *maîtrise* was 1,200 livres until 1776, when, as part of a general reduction, it was lowered to 900 livres. In Lyon and Marseille the fees were only slightly lower.[5] Large-scale producers of hats were usually the sons of merchants or professional men.[6]

5. Prices of membership of the various corporations can be found in Roze de Chantoiseau, *Essai sur l'Almanach général d'indication d'adresse personnelle et domicile fixe des six corps, arts et métiers* (Paris, 1769), and Garden, *Lyon et les Lyonnais,* 65.
6. Garden, *Lyon et les Lyonnais,* 63–65, 76–78.

It would be wrong, however, to assume from this that most of the journeymen who worked in Paris, Lyon, or Marseille remained journeymen all their lives in anything other than a purely formal sense or that their resources reflected the penury of a durably proletarian condition. Here the evidence supplied by marriage contracts is particularly difficult to interpret. In Lyon 80 percent of a sample of some three hundred journeymen in the hatting trade who married between 1786 and 1789 had assets of no more than 500 livres. Nearly half of them (46 percent) had less than 100 livres.[7] It is tempting to conclude that workers in the hatting trade were much less well endowed than journeymen in almost every other urban trade.[8] Yet the evidence is more ambiguous than it seems. In many of the urban trades marriage was often inseparable from the acquisition of a *maîtrise* and entry into the corporate world. As a result, many of the marriage contracts of journeymen tailors, shoemakers, joiners, or locksmiths were inflated by credit or by claims upon patrimonies that would be inherited at a future date. Journeymen in the hatting trade could not expect to acquire a *maîtrise* without working for many years to accumulate sufficient credit and capital to establish themselves on their own account. It is very likely therefore that the assets that went into the households they established were entirely their own and were not inflated by assets that had been promised or acquired on the basis of credit of one kind or another. It is probable that this situation, rather than any inherent lack of resources, is what marriage contracts reveal.

The likelihood that this was the case is reinforced by the substantially larger size of the assets of men described as

7. Ibid., 349.

8. This is the conclusion drawn by Garden (ibid.). His other claim, that levels of literacy among workers in the hatting trade were significantly lower than those of most journeymen (pp. 353, 450), is based upon a four-year sample of 258 marriage contracts taken from the period 1786–89. The figure (covering four years) represents under 10 percent of the labor force of the trade in a single year and its statistical significance is not clear. The activities of the journeymen described in the remainder of my study induce some skepticism.

ouvriers (rather than *compagnons*) *chapeliers*. On average the
value of their assets in late eighteenth-century Lyon was
some 750 livres.[9] It is probable that they were older men
who had spent some time working regularly in the trade
before they married. It is also possible that some of them did
not acquire a *maîtrise* at all and were able to establish themselves as small unincorporated artisans, repairing and selling hats, taking on subcontracted work as *apprêteurs*, or
making cheaper articles from wool or other materials on the
periphery of the trade.

The information in marriage contracts thus suggests that
there were temporal differences in the transfer of resources
from one generation to the next, as well as variations in the
opportunities available to the workforces of particular trades.
It is not easy, however, to establish how substantial or durable these differences might have been in the specific context
of the hatting trade. Much depended upon the composition
of the workforce. Many journeymen were migrants. There
were, however, various kinds of migrants. There were those
who had been sent by their families to serve an apprenticeship in one of the major centers of production and had remained there to work as journeymen. There were also itinerant journeymen who had learned the trade elsewhere but for
one reason or another had come to work in Paris, Lyon, or
Marseille. They too, of course, could become members of a
hatter's corporation, either by borrowing the money to pay
the required fee or by marrying the daughter or widow of an
established master. The proportion who did so was affected
by the state of the trade, the scale of migration, and the range
of available sources of credit.

A very incomplete enumeration of the journeymen working in the hatting trade of Marseille in 1782 or 1783 suggests
that under 20 percent of the workforce had been born in the
city or the area covered by its diocese.[10] By that date, how-

9. Ibid., 730.
10. A.C. Marseille, HH 399. The enumeration is not dated, but the
existence of several other enumerations carried out in 1782 and 1783 (as well
as the handwriting) suggests that it was done at the same time.

ever, it is likely that the proportion of migrants in the trade had increased substantially.[11] Nonetheless, it is very probable that a majority of those who worked in the hatting trades of Paris, Lyon, and Marseille had not been born there. The destinies of these different kinds of migrants were varied. Some of them may have returned to the small towns or villages where they had been born to practice the trade there in a small way. Others may have married and set themselves up on the periphery of the large urban trades, repairing or selling hats rather than making them or taking on subcontracted work on the finishing side of the trade. Here regularity and continuity of employment was particularly important. For work for wages was also a process of accumulating a nexus of kin, patrons, and friends as the basis of the credit needed not only to acquire membership of one or other of the corporations, but also to secure the viability of a small-scale hatting concern. The division between the core and the periphery of the trade has a particular significance in this context. Continuity of employment in the 15 to 20 percent of large enterprises where most journeymen worked was the key to access to a place among the 80 percent of small enterprises that formed the periphery of the trade.

From a journeyman's point of view, the periphery of the trade was a zone of opportunity where independent enterprises could be established. Here, there were several reasons why both large and small master hatters could afford to adopt a relatively relaxed attitude toward the provisions of corporate regulation governing entry to the trade. Although membership of a hatters' corporation was costly, the entry fee could be borrowed.[12] Hats to repair or sell were easily obtained at second or third hand and, at one time or another, most members of the public needed someone to repair and restore worn and shabby articles. In these circum-

11. See below, chapter 12.
12. For an example, A.D. Ville de Paris, D^5B^6 3692 (1776), where the outstanding sum on the 900-livre fee was paid in twelve promissory notes of 72 livres each.

stances, where the supply of raw materials was complemented by local markets for used goods, the advantages of corporate membership were more apparent for large manufacturers than small retailers. Membership of a corporation (as the census of the Parisian hatting trade in 1739 indicates) supplied them with regulated access to scarce materials, and to beaver in particular. Small retailers, on the other hand, had a variety of accessible sources of supply in the many intermediaries to whom the large enterprises sold their goods.

Large enterprises selling wholesale had few reasons for enforcing corporate regulations governing entry to the retail side of the trade. Since most large manufacturers' clients were other hatters or anyone else (mercers, hosiers, milliners, and the like) involved in the sale of hats to a final consumer, illegal entrants to the retail side of the trade were an irrelevance unless they dealt in stolen materials. There is little evidence that master hatters were particularly concerned by the presence of *ouvriers sans qualité*, or interlopers on the retail side of the trade.[13] Although wigmakers or tailors—or anyone involved in the sale of wine, meat, fruit, or vegetables—had good reason to fear unauthorized competition, the large hatting concerns could afford to turn a blind eye to journeymen dealing on their own account or repairing hats in a small way. The enforcement of corporate regulations governing entry to the trade occurred only when materials were scarce and theft was a matter of more than ordinary concern.

In normal circumstances, however, large entrepreneurs had little reason to take an active interest in the affairs of the periphery of the trade. Its existence enabled them to put out additional work on a subcontracted basis or lease the use of

13. The statement is based upon an examination of the scores of confiscations of goods from unauthorized retailers and (more rarely) manufacturers carried out in 1769–70 by the Parisian corporations and minuted in the papers of the *commissaires* of the Châtelet (A.N. Series Y). As one would expect, trades in which contact with a final consumer was particularly important (*vinaigriers, fruitiers-orangiers, limonadiers, tailleurs, merciers, menuisiers, lingères, fripiers, bonnetiers*, etc.) were particularly well represented. On attitudes toward the embezzlement of materials, see below, chapter 8.

their own equipment to small masters or journeymen. As a result, the line separating journeymen from the smaller master hatters who made up the large periphery of the main centers of production was not particularly distinct. The evidence on the condition of journeymen supplied by marriage contracts is therefore uncertain at best. It is likely that many of them, like workers in other eighteenth-century trades, saw work for wages as a temporary condition. It is also likely, however, that the process of escaping from wage labor in the hatting trade was more protracted than in other trades and may not always have entailed a change in formal status.[14] In these circumstances, journeymen in the hatting trade had a particular interest in ensuring that employment at the core was relatively stable and that access to the periphery remained within their grasp.

The division between the core and the periphery disclosed by the enumeration of 1739 is also apparent in the lists of workers drawn up by employers and returned to the authorities of the Parisian *sections* in 1790 and 1791 to establish how much small coin was needed to pay wages.[15] Although the returns are incomplete (only those for 41 of the 48 *sections* survive) and not entirely reliable, they contain a total of 67 manufacturers employing 1,602 workers. Here only 25 percent of all employers had fewer than ten workers, while 41 per cent employed twenty or more. The great

14. On differences between the ages of journeymen in the principal centers of production and those of migrants from elsewhere, see below, chapter 11. On subcontracted work and the lease of equipment, see Nollet, *L'Art de faire des chapeaux*, 39. Thus: "Il y a quantité d'ouvriers qui entreprennent des chapeaux et qui n'ont ni arçons ni fourneaux; ceux-là vont faire leur ouvrage dans les ateliers où il n'y a point assez de compagnons pour remplir toutes les places; ce qui se paye pour cela aux maîtres les dédommage de la perte qu'ils feroient s'ils allumoient leurs fourneaux avec un trop petit nombre d'ouvriers." In Paris in the early 1760s the fee paid to use an *arçon* was a sou; the fee for felting a hat was 5 sous. On journeymen's ambivalent attitudes toward subcontracted work, see below, chapters 7 and 11.

15. Figures have been calculated from the ones printed by F. Braesch, "Essai de statistique de la population ouvrière parisienne en 1790 et 1791," *La Révolution française* 6 (1913): 162–224, which, despite its imperfections, is an adequate basis for calculating the bipartite structure presented here.

Table 3   Distribution of Employment by Workshop Size
in the Parisian Hatting Trade, 1790–91

Workers per Shop	Masters	Journeymen
0–4	0	0
5–9	17	113
10–19	22	273
20–39	13	290
40+	15	926
Total	67	1,602

Source: F. Braesch, "Essai de statistique de la population ouvrière parisienne en 1790 et 1791," *La Révolution française* 6 (1913): 162–224.

majority of those employed (75.9 per cent) worked in *fabriques* containing twenty or more other workers. Over half the workforce (58 percent) was employed by fifteen manufacturers (table 3).

Too much significance should not be drawn from what appears to have been a massive increase in the number employed and a substantial concentration of the labor force into larger units of production between the two enumerations. The list drawn up in 1739 did not include the large number of women who worked in the trade; it was also drawn up after many journeymen had been laid off because of the shortage of beaver. At most it suggests that, in normal circumstances, the gulf between the core and the periphery of the trade was even more pronounced than the census of 1739 indicates. As in most trades, changes in the size of the workforce during periods of recession tended to occur within the larger enterprises.[16]

It would be naive to expect a linear process of concentration to have occurred in a trade as subject to fluctuations in the supply of materials and the vagaries of international markets as the hatting trade. There is no reason to suppose that patterns of employment and fluctuations in the size of the workforce were any more stable or regular than they

16. For examples from other trades, see Sonenscher, *Work and Wages*.

were in most eighteenth-century trades.[17] The only surviving evidence of the scale of these fluctuations is to be found in the records of the unsuccessful hatting concern established at Rennes. Production figures exist for seven months between April 1782 and January 1783 when the establishment had become very small. They reveal variations of a scale that can be explained only by the addition of one or two more journeymen to the firm's tiny workforce (table 4).

A more significant detail disclosed by these figures is the absence of any relationship between output figures and gross monthly wage payments. Erratic work rhythms in an unsuccessful venture may have contributed something to this pattern, but it can be explained more easily in terms of the number of intermediate processes involved in the production of hats. This meant that a hatting concern was obliged to pay workers who were not involved in the production of the final product. In this, the hatting trade was relatively unusual. In most eighteenth-century trades many intermediate processes were subcontracted out to other master artisans.[18] In the hatting trade only the dyeing process was subcontracted out and, as the example of the only relatively large concern in mid-eighteenth century Rouen indicates, even this stage was often integrated into the enterprise.[19]

Although the size and capital requirements of large hatting enterprises present some similarities to those of medium-sized textile concerns, the various phases of the productive process in the hatting trade were much more integrated. This relatively high level of integration, and the resultant inability

17. On the tailoring trade, see Michael Sonenscher, "Journeymen's Migrations and Workshop Organization in Eighteenth-Century France: The Tailors of Rouen," in Kaplan and Koepp, Work in France, 74–96. On printing, see R. C. Darnton, The Business of Enlightenment (Cambridge, Mass., 1979), 177–245, and The Literary Underground of the Old Regime (Cambridge, Mass., 1982), 148–66; Jacob Rychner, Genève et ses typographes vus de Neuchâtel (Geneva, 1985).

18. Some discussion of the problem is presented in Michael Sonenscher, "The Sans-Culottes of the Year II: Rethinking the Language of Labour in Revolutionary France," Social History 9 (1984): 301–28; see also Work and Wages, for a fuller discussion.

19. See above, p. 41, table 1.

Table 4   Production and Wage Payments
in Rennes, 1782–83

Month	Number of Hats	Monthly Wages (livres/sous/deniers)	Wages per Hat (livres)
April	69	302 10 9	4.4
May	89	202 0 3	2.3
August	96	371 14 0	3.9
September	56	263 11 0	4.7
October	59	301 17 3	5.1
December	219	414 10 0	1.9
January	211	404 13 3	1.9

Source: A.D. Ile-et-Vilaine, C 1512–13.

of manufacturers to devolve the costs of producing stocks of unfinished goods onto subcontractors, was one crucial reason why the trade responded very rapidly to changes in the price of materials and why its response took the form of attempts to modify working practices. Wages were the largest single item in the ordinary monthly expenditure of large hatting concerns.[20] While the supply and price of materials were largely beyond their control, wage rates and working arrangements were not. If prices rose, hatting firms were obliged to carry the additional costs of materials into markets where prices were also set by English or Dutch competitors. In these circumstances, there were strong pressures to economize on labor costs.

Both the size of the workforce and the relatively high level of liquidity required to meet the wage costs associated with structurally integrated intermediate processes were not confined to the Parisian trade. The size of the larger workshops in the capital, with their forty or more journeymen and a further score of women workers, was matched by that of establishments in Lyon and Marseille. The trade in Lyon was said to include over eighty *fabricants* in 1747.[21] Figures of

20. Wages accounted for over 50 percent of the monthly expenditure of one Parisian hatter in 1784 (A.D. Ville de Paris, D⁵B⁶ 1983).

21. A.D. Rhône, 3E 7891 (94) (27 February 1747).

the number of workers are imprecise. A list made in 1743 of all the apprentices, journeymen, clerks, and sons of masters required to serve in the militia amounted to no more than 270 individuals.[22] Married men, journeymen not settled in Lyon, and women were clearly excluded. In 1777 there were said to be 1,500 *compagnons* or *ouvriers* employed in the trade, while Déglize produced a total of 4,873 workers in his census of the trade in 1789.[23] The 70 manufacturers he counted employed 2,504 felters and finishers and a further 275 apprentices—an average of nearly 40 male workers per unit of production—as well as a further 1,114 women.[24]

The dimensions of the trade in Marseille were similar. A levy of a sou a week on everyone in the trade—masters, journeymen, and apprentices—was farmed out in 1710 for 870 livres a year, a sum that suggests a figure of some three hundred individuals in the trade.[25] In 1718 there were seventy-three masters in Marseille.[26] After the catastrophe of the plague in 1720 the number of masters returned to figures of seventy and seventy-nine in 1733 and 1749 respectively. A description of the state of manufacture in Marseille in 1760 referred to forty *fabriques* employing an estimated five hundred workers.[27] A list of masters and journeymen fit to carry arms and take part in the procession held in honor of the visit of the comte de Provence in 1777 contains the names of 52 manufacturers and 343 workers. Again women, for obvious reasons, were excluded from the list and it is probable that only journeymen who were domiciled or in stable employment in the city were recorded. As a result, the number of journeymen listed is something of an understatement (table 5). An incomplete enumeration of the number of journeymen employed by thirty-eight *fabricants* shortly be-

22. Ibid., 3E 7887 (344) (6 September 1743).
23. A.N. F^{12} 763; A.C. Lyon, I^2 46 bis, fol. 113. On these figures, see also Garden, *Lyon et les Lyonnais*, 317–18.
24. Garden, *Lyon et les Lyonnais*, 322.
25. A.D. Bouches-du-Rhône, 366E^{237} (11 July 1710).
26. Ibid., 366E^{241} (28 May 1718).
27. A.N. K 907.

Table 5   Distribution of Employment in
the Hatting Trade of Marseille, 1777

Number of Masters	Number of Journeymen Employed
20	1–4
21	5–9
6	10–14
3	15–19
1	20–29
1	30–49
Total 52	343

Source: A.D. Bouches-du-Rhône, 367E²⁶⁸, fol. 615v (10 June 1777).

Table 6   Distribution of Employment in
the Hatting Trade of Marseille, ca. 1783

Number of Masters	Number of Journeymen Employed
13	1–4
11	5–9
7	10–14
4	15–19
3	20–29

Source: A.C. Marseille, HH 399.

fore 1789 provides a similar profile (table 6). At that time the corporation consisted of eighty-eight masters and six widows.[28] A memorandum produced in 1803 stated that there had been sixty manufacturers employing some eight hundred men and four hundred women in Marseille on the eve of the Revolution.[29]

These figures are best taken as rough indications of the magnitude of hatting concerns in the eighteenth century. They underline the importance of relatively large establishments throughout the century. The capital required on this

28. A.C. Marseille, HH 399.
29. P. Masson, *Les Bouches-du-Rhône: Encyclopédie départementale* (Paris, 1926), 8:4.

side of the trade was of comparable magnitude. The price of a merchant hatter's shop in Paris in 1778, including utensils, goods, and equipment, amounted to no more than 3,815 livres, including 2,615 livres for the stock; the equipment of the manufactory in Rennes, designed for thirty felters, was valued at 5,000 livres in 1776 and reduced in 1784 to a mere 1,248 livres. But the sums invested in some partnerships were comparable to those invested in textile houses.[30] The Parisian firm of Chol et Cie, reputedly the second most prestigious house in the capital, was established in 1752 with a capital of 40,000 livres, half of which came from the partnership of Maurice and Antoine Giraud of Lyon.[31] It was succeeded by the firm of Chol et Janin in 1763 and was still in existence over twenty years later. The latter partnership was also a limited one (*société en commandite*), with 60,000 of its capital of 120,000 livres supplied on a limited liability basis by Giraud from Lyon.[32] Another *société en commandite* was established in 1751. Trading under the name of Dame Descordes et Cie, it had an initial capital of 50,000 livres, 30,000 of which came from two Parisian rentiers.[33]

The scale of business of partnerships such as these was comparable to that of a medium-sized textile firm. The partnership of Vourlat et Charton of Lyon, established in 1742 and terminated in 1748 after the death of one of the partners, had outstanding assets in the form of unpaid debts worth 90,000 livres. The firm's equipment was valued at 3,000 livres and its stock of pelts, fur, and unsold hats a further 36,000 livres.[34] Its debtors were distributed all over France, with extensions eastward to Geneva, Basel, and Zu-

30. A.N. Y 11 019[b] (2 July 1778); A.D. Ile-et-Vilaine, C 1513 (28 January 1784); B.H.V.P. MS. CP 4858, *journal* of Petit aîné et Cie (1763–65).
31. A.D. Ville de Paris, D³B⁶ 53 (8 March 1752).
32. Ibid., D³B⁶ 64 (19 September 1763).
33. Ibid., D³B⁶ 52 (1 September 1751).
34. A.D. Rhône, 3E 9685 (19 October 1748). The trade could also result in the accumulation of relatively substantial fortunes. Etienne Mazard, one of the partners in the largest hatting concern in Lyon in the early eighteenth century, left 135,000 livres to the Hôpital de la charité when he died (Garden, *Lyon et les Lyonnais*, 394).

rich. Firms of this size fitted easily into the extensive circuits of credit involved in both the acquisition of materials and the sale of manufactured goods that were characteristic of eighteenth-century commercial life. Cash was often a problem, particularly in periods of intense activity before orders were sent out to coincide with the departure of merchant ships or the Manila galleon to the Spanish colonies. At times like this, firms needed to get rid of unsold stock as quickly as possible to generate the liquidity needed to pay wages. If they could not, the money was borrowed on relatively long credit (of eight to nine months) or the loan was set against the (suitably discounted) price of the unsold goods.[35]

Credit was therefore an integral component of the economy of hat production. In itself this was not exceptional; credit was the lifeblood of the urban trades as a whole. The scale and extent of chains of credit were, however, much larger in the hatting trade than in many others. The usual hazards of buying and selling on credit (especially to aristocratic customers) were compounded by the dimensions of the international market, the relatively high levels of wage costs on intermediate processes and, most importantly, by the substantial outlays required to maintain adequate stocks of beaver.

Beaver was by far the most costly of the materials used in the production of hats. Beaver pelts were sold by the pound; the pelts of the other animals used most frequently in the trade sold by the quintal, equivalent to a hundred pounds. In 1733 the Compagnie des Indes was selling beaver pelts at 3 livres 10 sous a pound for parchment beaver and 5 livres 10 sous for coat beaver.[36] Muscovy pelts sold at 4 livres 10

---

35. "J'aurois bien souhaité que vous m'eussiez pu vendre chez vous une partie de ces chapeaux pour me faire un peu de fondz, qui me manquent ordinairement dans le temps des dépêches de flotte ou gallion à cause du grand débit que je fais. . . . Si vous pourriez m'avancer pour 8 à 9 mois 4 à 500 écus je vous seray obligé et je vous payerai l'intérêt comme vous le trouverez à propos, ou vous les prendrez sur les premiers de mes retours qui vous viendront." A.D. Ville de Paris, D⁵B⁶ 2152, Antoine Mathieu to Philippe Deschamps (7 June 1735).

36. B.M. Rouen, MS. 884ᵇ; see too A.D. Rhône, 3E 7879 (266) (19 September 1735).

sous a pound. A seven-ounce beaver hat sold in Paris for between 20 and 22 livres at the same time.[37]

Prices rose considerably thereafter. Between 1744 and 1753 a pound of good-quality pelts rose from 6 livres 10 sous to 8 livres and was over a third higher still at the end of the Seven Years' War when direct access to supplies from North America was finally lost.[38] The level of 12 livres a pound appears to have remained fairly constant until the American War. Rumors of war sent prices higher. In December 1778 a pound of finest-quality beaver fur was reported to have sold for 64 livres.[39] In 1779 a Parisian hatter was still able to pay his correspondent in Saint-Malo 12 livres for a pound of beaver pelts, but prices increased sharply in the course of the war.[40] By the early 1780s beaver pelts were selling in Paris at 16 livres a pound, while a pound of beaver fur cost over 48 livres.[41] Even the financially straitened *manufacture royale* in Rennes was able to dispose of its surplus stocks of beaver fur to a Parisian hatter for between 48 and 52 livres a pound. The price of the principal material used to make fine-quality hats thus increased by over 300 percent between the early 1730s and the late 1770s, or more than three times the average increase in the wholesale price of corn. As beaver fur became increasingly scarce and expensive, other materials became increasingly attractive. By way of comparison, rabbit pelts were selling at 35 to 42 livres a quintal and hare for between 72 and 100 livres a quintal in the early 1780s.[42] Beaver pelts and beaver fur were between ten and fifty times more costly.

37. Ibid.

38. Nollet, *L'Art de faire des chapeaux*, 9; B.H.V.P. MS. CP 4858.

39. A.D. Ile-et-Vilaine, C 1510 (18 December 1778). Some of the manufactory's imported pelts were purchased from the firm of Loubier, Teissier, et Cie of London (ibid., 2 April 1778). There was also an extensive traffic in *lie de vin*, centered upon Orléans, Blois, and Tours in the case of the Parisian hatting trade (ibid., 2 December 1778).

40. A.D. Ville de Paris, D^5B^6 98, *Journal*, J. Perrin.

41. A.D. Ile-et-Vilaine, C 1509 (13 October 1779); A.D. Ville de Paris, D^5B^6 1983, *Livre d'achats*, Leconte.

42. A.D. Ville de Paris, D^5B^6 1983, *Livre d'achats*, Leconte.

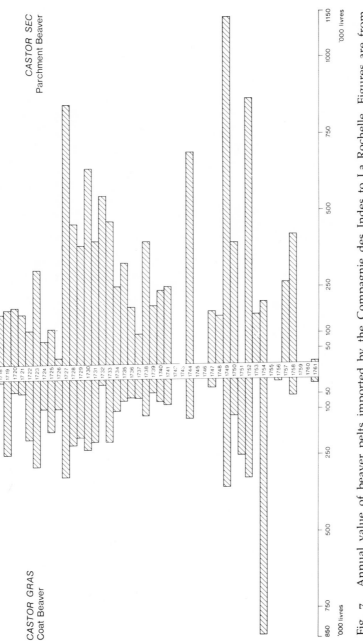

Fig. 7. Annual value of beaver pelts imported by the Compagnie des Indes to La Rochelle. Figures are from Archives de la Chambre de Commerce, La Rochelle, carton 27; and Emile Garnault, *Le Commerce rochelais: Les Rochelais et le Canada* (La Rochelle, 1893), 15–16.

Even before the loss of Canada, imports of beaver pelts by the Compagnie des Indes appear to have fluctuated and were particularly vulnerable to wartime disruption. Since the duty on imported pelts was levied on the basis of a standard price, the figures of the value of imported pelts are a guide to the volume of imports (fig. 7). The census of journeymen employed in the Parisian trade in 1739 was a response to a severe shortage of beaver resulting from the low level of imports in the preceding years. In February of that year the hatters of Lyon complained that they had had no beaver pelts for six months. The industry, they stated, usually produced eight to ten different sorts of hats, which were sold in assorted bales in France and Spain. Orders had already been placed by their correspondents for the required assortments, which usually consisted of seven or eight dozen beaver hats for every forty or fifty dozen hats in the bale. The normal annual consumption of beaver in Lyon amounted to 278 bales of pelt; even the little that had been sent belatedly by the Compagnie des Indes contained too many pelts from which the fur had been shaved. As a result, they claimed, it was likely that the Spanish market would be lost to the English.[43]

As figure 7 demonstrates, shortages and gluts were an increasingly regular occurrence during the following two decades. Neither state of affairs had its advantages. Shortages meant higher prices; gluts meant the risk of unused quantities of perishable—and ultimately worm-ridden—pelts. Dependence upon supplies of beaver meant vulnerability to the vagaries of the military and political situation in North America in the short term and exposure to the steeply rising price of beaver pelts, magnified by the loss of Canada after 1761, in the long term. The relatively high level of integra-

43. A.D. Rhône, 3E 7883 (11 February 1739). According to the hatters of Lyon, the shortage had been caused "par le peu de ménagement que les agents de la Compagnie dans le Canada y ont pour les sauvages. Ceux-cy, rebutés de leur procédé, se sont insensiblement tournés du côté des anglais et ils leur portent leurs pelleteries."

tion of the process of hatmaking meant that it was impossible to escape the upward pressure upon costs by devolving them onto subcontractors. Instead, firms began a gradual and, ultimately, successful attempt to replace the fur of the beaver by that of other animals. This process had widespread effects, however, upon the organization of work.

6

Trade Secrets

Whatever the differences and particularities that separated them, hatters in Paris, Lyon, and Marseille—the major urban centers of the trade in the second half of the eighteenth century—consciously shared situations and concerns that were closely related to the use and availability of beaver fur. Their solution to the problem of the rising price of beaver took two related forms.

The first found its expression in the piecemeal dissemination of minor changes in the techniques of hat production. Although these modifications did not amount to anything that could be dignified as a technological revolution, they do demonstrate that the relatively static technologies of the eighteenth century were not, in themselves, obstacles to changes in the organization of work and increases in the productivity of labor. As a result, the history of the eighteenth-century French hatting trade also discloses an aspect of artisanal production that is somewhat different from the small-scale, stable, custom-bound image usually associated with pre-industrial forms of manufacture.

Changes in productivity in the hatting trade came about by substituting labor-saving materials for labor-intensive materials—or, more concretely, by substituting hare for beaver fur as the principal material from which hats were made. The great advantage of coat beaver was its felting capacity. The grease and sweat embedded in the fur of the coats worn by North American Indians made it possible to produce high-quality, long-lasting hats without the assistance of a felting agent. Other furs, including parchment beaver, felted less easily, and hatters mixed in small amounts of coat beaver with them to facilitate the process. When supplies of coat beaver began to become scarce and it became necessary to find a way of producing good felt from the stiff and brittle fur of the hare, hatting firms developed their own preparation to reproduce the effects of coat beaver. This preparation was known as a special solution, or *eau de composition*, and, more ambiguously, as a *secret*.

The word *secret* or *secrétage* evoked, as contemporaries were well aware, both the mystery of the specific ingredients used in the preparation of the solution and the power of the solution to secrete substances that encouraged fur to felt.[1] The preparation was initially a mixture of water and nitric or sulphuric acid (*eau forte* or *esprit de vitriol*) and was applied to the pelts of rabbits to allow the fur to be removed more easily. During the latter half of the eighteenth century, it also came to be used to enhance the limited felting propensity of hare fur. The addition of tallow and mercury to the solution made it possible to produce a felt that, it was claimed, was as strong and durable as beaver felt.

There were also attempts to abandon the use of the fur of animals altogether. In 1764 a master hatter from Marseille claimed that he had found a way of making hats from cotton wool (*apoçin*), costing 2 livres a pound instead of the 30 livres that a pound of beaver fur cost.[2] It was hare, however,

1. "Le terme de *secret* et de *secréter* prouve en même temps qu'il vient du mystère que tous les chapeliers ont fait de cet apprêt, et de la variété de leur méthode et la préférence que chacun d'eux donne à la sienne." *Encyclopédie méthodique: Manufactures, arts, et métiers* (Paris, 1787), 1:153. According to the anonymous author of this article, the procedure had been known in France before the revocation of the Edict of Nantes in 1685 and had been reintroduced to the trade by a French hatter named Mathieu, who had worked in London. According to the hatters' corporation of Lyon, in 1735 "le chapeau du secret se fabrique avec du seul poil de lièvre et du lapin. Mais comme ce poil de sa nature n'est pas propre à faire un bon feutre parce qu'il est trop sec et qu'il n'est point liant, on fait une composition remplie d'ingrédiens tels que l'eau forte, graisse de mulet, esprit de vitriol etc. dont on frotte le poil de lièvre et de lapin sur sa peau." A.D. Rhône, 3E 7879 (266) (19 September 1735).

2. His claim was disputed by the hatters' corporation and a lawsuit followed (Archives de la Chambre de commerce de Marseille, H 212, "Mémoire pour la communauté des marchands fabricans de chapeaux de Mar-

that was favored most widely. In 1770, to reduce the growing pressure upon domestic supplies, the Crown doubled the duty levied on exported pelts. By the mid-1780s demand for hare had risen to such a level that the hatters' corporation of Lyon was obliged to petition the Crown for a total embargo upon the export of pelts.[3] The attractions of hare were considerable. It was cheap. Above all, the substitution of hare for beaver fur made it possible to produce between 30 and 40 percent more hats a week.

The second aspect of the solution to the problem of the price of beaver was closely related to the first. The use of hare to make hats was illegal. The dissemination of minor changes in techniques thus implied major changes in the relationship between the law and the trade. The process found its expression in regular, if at times hesitant, coordination of corporate regulation and in repeated attempts to use the law and the courts—the Chambre de police of the Châtelet of Paris, the Consulat of Lyon, the Echevinage of Marseille, together with the two Parlements of Paris and Aix—to divest the work that journeymen performed of an identity that derived from the tradition of natural law.

The implications of these developments were substantial. Hare was less costly and more easily obtained than beaver fur. As a result, the threshold of entry into the core of the large urban hatting trades fell. Ease of access to a cheaper material was reinforced by a reduction in the formal barriers to entry to the trade. A series of rulings by the Conseil d'état after 1762 removed many restrictions upon the production of manufactured goods in rural areas.[4] Established firms thus

---

seille contre le nommé Jordani" [Paris, 1766] and "A Monseigneur le Contrôleur-Général des Finances" [Paris, 1766]).

3. A.D. Ile-et-Vilaine, C 1508 (16 September 1770); A.N. F^{12} 203–4 (June 1785 and 30 May 1786).

4. Printed copies of the *arrêts* (7 September 1762; 13 February 1765; 28 February 1766), which concerned textile production rather than hats but whose implications were clear, can be found in the John Crerar Library Collection housed in the University of Chicago Library (callmarks 883, 887, 888). On hats, see A.N. AB XIX 669^a (28 February 1766).

faced the prospect of competition from new entrants to the trade and from rural manufacturers in particular. The effects of the entry of competing firms into the hatting trade are visible in the long-term stability of the price of high-quality hats between the early 1730s and the early 1780s. In the earlier period, the price of a seven- or eight-ounce beaver hat was said to be some 22 livres.[5] By 1785 the price of the best-quality hats produced in both Lyon and the little town of Anduze in the Cévennes ranged from 12 to 24 livres.[6] The substitution of hare for beaver fur was matched by the transformation of villages like Chazelles-sur-Lyon and Tence, both near Lyon, and Camps-la-Source, near Marseille, into considerable proto-industrial centers.[7] By 1789 it was reported that there were 48 small hatting enterprises and some 450 workers, each making a thousand hats a year (or an average of three a day) in Chazelles alone.[8]

The emergence of these centers of production also created a substantial opportunity to transfer part of the process of production from the towns to the countryside. Rural producers did not pay urban rents or buy all the items that they needed for their daily consumption. In addition, the use of hare instead of beaver fur meant that the pool of labor available to large hatting enterprises was potentially very much larger. Skill was linked to materials. The journeymen who worked on the felting side of the trade in Paris, Lyon, and Marseille were valued because of their familiarity with beaver fur.[9] When beaver was no longer used, there were good reasons for transferring the felting side of the trade from the towns to the countryside. Not only did this move

5. B.M. Rouen, MS. 884[b].

6. A.D. Gard, 1 Mi. 90 (R 1).

7. Edmond Ortigue and Raymond Rolland, "Les Chapeliers de Camps-la-Source," *Etudes rurales* 93–94 (1984): 243–70; Eliane Bolomier, "La Chapellerie à Chazelles: Esquisse chronologique," ibid., 271–76. For the development of another (nineteenth-century) zone of rural production, see Serge Moscovici, *Réconversion industrielle et changements sociaux: La chapellerie dans l'Aude* (Paris, 1961).

8. Bolomier, "La Chapellerie," 272; A.C. Lyon, I[2] 46 bis, fol. 113 et seq.

9. See above, chapter 4.

make it possible to devolve the heavy current costs of wage payments onto subcontractors (and, in this way, bring the capital structure of the hatting trade into line with the textile trades), it also opened urban labor markets to journeymen who had never made hats from beaver fur.

Journeymen who worked on the felting side of the trade were paid by the piece. The rates varied according to the type of hat they produced. Generally the rates for making a hat from beaver fur were twice as high as those for making hats from other materials, because the fulling process was twice as long. Six or seven hours were needed to turn beaver fur into a malleable felt, but only three hours were required to produce felt from other materials and from hare in particular.[10] The use of hare introduced a new element into established scales of piece rates. Initially, the substantially lower costs of the fur made it possible for large firms to pay journeymen the prevailing rates for making beaver hats even though their work had become very much less labor-intensive. As a result, it is very probable that, at certain times during the decade between 1750 and 1760, journeymen were able to earn more and work less than they had done previously or would do subsequently.

In the longer term, however, the lower threshold of entry into the trade, the gradual transfer of the felting stage of the production process to rural areas, and the resultant emergence of a larger pool of labor all combined to ensure that workers making hats from hare could not be paid at the same rates as workers making hats from beaver. The substitution of hare for beaver fur placed considerable pressures upon master hatters in the principal centers of urban production to bring the piece rates they paid for hats made mainly from hare fur into line with the rates paid for other ordinary hats. In itself, this reduction in piece rates need not have affected the weekly sums that journeymen earned. The higher levels of productivity associated with hare meant that

10. A.D. Rhône, 3E 7879 (19 September 1735).

journeymen would have earned as much if they were prepared to make a larger number of hats. Yet, until well into
the nineteenth century they refused to make more than two
hats a day, even though it was technically possible to make
a larger number.

There were several reasons for this apparently contradictory attitude. The first had to do with the composition of the
hats themselves. Most hats were not made entirely of hare
or entirely of beaver but contained different amounts of various kinds of fur. Both the time needed to produce a malleable felt and the rates at which the work was paid were
therefore open to different interpretations. Here, the composition of the hats known as half-beavers (*demi-castors*) was
particularly contentious, because the identity of the hats was
closely related to the concerns of the journeymen who made
them.

The substitution of hare for beaver fur also affected the
relationship between journeymen working in the core of the
urban hatting trades and their chances of finding a place
among the large number of tiny enterprises that formed its
periphery. As in most trades, the hatting trades of Paris,
Lyon, and Marseille consisted of a small core of large enterprises where the majority (or a large minority) of journeymen worked.[11] Regular employment in the core of the trade
was the key to the limited possibilities available to journeymen to enter the periphery of the trade as small retailers or
hat repairers. Here, lack of familiarity with the use of beaver
fur was a technical obstacle to the entry of journeymen from
other localities into the trade. As the use of hare became
more widespread, the size of the pool of labor available to
produce hats became more substantial. Journeymen in the
hatting trades of the major urban centers of production were
faced with an increasing number of potential competitors for
employment. At the same time the large hatting enterprises,
faced with competition from rural producers, were obliged

11. See above, chapter 5.

either to raise their output levels or to subcontract the felting side of the production process out to rural manufacturers or to employ journeymen who were prepared to make more than two hats a day.

The increase in the supply of labor indicates why journeymen working in the core of the urban trades were likely to regard outsiders with some suspicion. Outsiders were a potential threat to regular employment and an obstacle to the protracted process of accumulating sufficient wealth to establish a small enterprise. The increase in the supply of labor does not, however, explain why established journeymen refused to make more than two hats a day. In fact, it makes their refusal all the more puzzling. To understand why they did so, two further aspects of the work of making hats require consideration. The first is the distinctive pattern of work followed by journeymen on the felting side of the trade. The second, which applied to both felters and finishers, concerns the schedules of production of the trade as a whole.

The process of making felt consisted of two stages. In the first stage journeymen separated and untangled the fibers of measured amounts of fur by passing the vibrating cord of a bowing instrument, or *arçon*, through small piles of the raw material. During the second stage journeymen "built" the hat by placing the conically shaped piles of fur on top of one another before kneading and pressing them over a heated solution to form a felt (see above, figures 2–4). During the eighteenth century this work was done by two men who worked in pairs. They did not, however, divide the labor between one another. This was because they were paid for each hat, and for this reason the wages they earned were the "price" of making a hat. It is clear, in other words, that the conventions of a tradition of civil jurisprudence rather than any technical obstacle placed limits upon the extent of the division of labor. As a result, the normal pattern of work consisted of a sequence of alternating roles. While one man used the *arçon* to prepare the fur, the other formed his *capades* into the shape of a hat. This pattern ensured that each journeyman worked only on his "own" materials.[12] The pattern of a working day can be presented schematically as follows (where A and B are two journeymen):

Bowing	*Felting*
A	B
B	A
A	B
B	A

Thus, at the end of the day journeyman A would have made two hats. Journeyman B would have made one hat and prepared the fur for completion on the following day.

This was the usual pattern of work that journeymen on the felting side of the trade followed. It explains why, in 1773, the hatters of Lyon produced the somewhat bewildering statement that although journeymen made no more than two hats a day, they produced only nine hats a week.[13] By working in pairs, each journeyman's weekly output would have had the following pattern:

	Mon.	*Tues.*	*Wed.*	*Thurs.*	*Fri.*	*Sat.*
Journeyman A	1	2	1	2	1	2
Journeyman B	2	1	2	1	2	1

Since the time needed to carry out the processes of bowing, forming the *capades*, and making felt from the fur of hare treated with the *eau de composition* was substantially lower than the time needed to perform the same operations using beaver fur, it would seem that it was possible to accommodate the production of an additional hat without affecting the length of the working day. A twelve-hour working day—the time required to make two beaver hats—was, it

12. As Nollet put it in his *L'Art de faire des chapeaux*, 38–39, "Comme chaque compagnon commence et finit les chapeaux qu'il entreprend, il faut qu'il partage son temps entre la foule et les autres façons qui la précèdent."
13. A.C. Lyon, HH 32, "Mémoire des maîtres chapeliers" (September 1773). See also chapter 8 below.

would seem, an adequate period to make three hats from hare fur since they needed only three hours each to produce. It would seem therefore that the production of two hats a day, or nine hats a week, from hare fur implied a working day of some four to six hours.[14]

In fact this was not the case. For journeymen did more than make hats. A substantial part of the working day was given over to unloading and moving timber or charcoal for the fires used to heat the felting solution, to mixing required amounts of water and wine waste into fulling vats, to lighting fires or delivering and collecting materials. Nollet, in his remarks on the Parisian hatting trade, published in *L'Art de faire des chapeaux* (1765), produced a description of a journeyman's working week that, although less uniform than the one presented schematically above, conforms to the same pattern. Mondays and Tuesdays, he wrote, were given over to the work of bowing and building the hats. The remainder of the week was used to turn the conically shaped *capades* into felt, which was then molded into the shape of the hats. Even on those days, however, two or three hours were needed to prepare the fulling vats, so that the work of making the hats themselves only began at ten or eleven o'clock in the morning.[15]

None of these activities were covered by the rates at which journeymen were paid. Journeymen were paid for what they made rather than for what they did. It is clear, however, that they did a great deal more than make hats. Yet their wages were set as if this was all they did. The pattern of work that they followed also echoed this assumption. Each individual worked on "his" materials and was paid for "his" hat. The ancillary work of preparing the vats

14. The hours have been calculated from A.C. Marseille, FF 386 (13 August 1776), and A.D. Rhône, 3E 7879 (19 September 1735).

15. "On ne foule guère le Lundi; ni même le Mardi. Les compagnons emploient ces deux jours-là tout entiers à arçonner et à bastir afin d'avoir de l'avance pour les jours suivants; dans le reste de la semaine il est presque toujours 10 à 11 heures dans la matinée avant qu'ils se mettent à fouler, parce qu'il faut bien deux ou trois heures pour mettre le bain en état." Nollet, *L'Art de faire des chapeaux*, 38.

and mixing the felting solution was done in turn.[16] As a result, each individual was paid for what he made, while everyone participated in work that was not paid at all.

The form of the wage and the pattern of work in the hatting trade embodied the prevailing conventions of the tradition of natural law. Journeymen had rights in their labor and expended that labor in transforming the materials supplied to them by their masters. The wage was, quite literally, *le prix de la façon d'un chapeau*, the price of making a hat. Since they were paid for what they made rather than for what they did, it was they who managed the allocation of their time between paid and unpaid work. For as long as the wage embodied the assumption that journeymen had rights of property in their labor, so that work and working time were not identical, there was a clear logic in their refusal to make more than two hats a day.

This logic arose from the arrangements that the journeymen made to allocate their time between paid and unpaid work in an equitable manner. Since the working day consisted of both paid and unpaid work, cooperation over the allocation of unpaid time depended upon the preservation of a pattern of work that allowed each individual to make the same number of hats in the course of a week. The journeymen's refusal to make more than two hats a day was based on a fear that a higher level of output would lead to an inequitable distribution of unpaid work. It would mean that some individuals made more hats than others and that the arrangements allowing them to work in pairs would become impossible.

16. "Quand ils sont plusieurs, ils doivent s'entendre pour aller ensemble, afin que le fourneau une fois allumé serve pour tous à la fois. . . . Un des compagnons à tour de rôle allume le fourneau, fait chauffer l'eau, prépare le bain en y mettant la quantité de lie qu'il faut. . . . Et quand tout cela est fait il en donne avis à ses camarades qui apportent leurs *Bastissages* et qui se placent le long des deux bancs [i.e., workbenches] suivant leur rang d'ancienneté dans la fabrique où ils travaillent, car comme les bancs sont beaucoup plus longs que la chaudière, ceux qui ont droit d'occuper le milieu sont plus avantageusement placés." Nollet, *L'Art de faire des chapeaux*, 39.

The need to preserve a uniform level of weekly output was the more necessary, from a journeyman's point of view, because of the schedules of production of the trade as a whole. Although they worked in pairs, the journeymen who worked on the felting side of the trade were not taken on in pairs. Nor did each pair take its turn to felt the materials that had been prepared. As Nollet pointed out, access to the workbenches where the fur was felted was organized in terms of an informal hierarchy of seniority.[17] The men who had been employed the longest in any particular enterprise were entitled to first use of the felting vats. Yet the composition of an enterprise's workforce was—as it was in any eighteenth-century trade—relatively unstable. Journeymen were taken on or laid off to meet the erratic schedules that were the hallmark of batch rather than serial production. From year to year a proportion of the output of the hatting trades of Paris, Lyon, and Marseille was destined for markets beyond the frontiers, so that schedules of production followed the rhythms of orders and the episodic surges of demand arising from the impending departure of merchant ships, or were synchronized to meet the calendars of the great fairs of Beaucaire, Caen, and Guibray where many wholesale transactions were conducted throughout the eighteenth century.[18]

By limiting output to two hats a day, journeymen were able to secure a relatively stable level of income for the constantly changing pairs of individuals employed on the felting side of the trade. At the same time, they could spread the effects of sharp increases in demand among the wide number of individuals, with whom, at one time or another, they were obliged to work. In this sense, a stable set of working arrangements was a counterpart to the fluidity and uncertainties of local labor markets. It allowed journeymen to reconcile the differences in age, seniority, and length of

17. Places along the workbenches were allocated "suivant leur rang d'ancienneté dans la fabrique" (ibid.).
18. See above, chapter 4.

employment that existed among them with a pattern of work that was not an obstacle to an adequate income.

The changes in productivity that accompanied the use of hare also affected the relationship between the different groups of workers involved in the production of hats. Most importantly, the relationship between felters and finishers (*fouleurs* and *approprieurs*) was transformed. Finishing a hat was always a more delicate but less time-consuming and labor-intensive activity than making one. One *approprieur* was needed to finish the hats made by five or six *fouleurs*. Higher productivity on the felting side of the trade meant a larger quantity of hats to be finished and a greater demand for finishers, particularly because hats made of hare, however they had been treated, were not as strong as hats made from beaver. The bottleneck was made the more acute as a proportion of the felting side of the trade was transferred to rural areas. A master hatter from Lyon, writing in 1781, recorded (with some exaggeration) that workers on the finishing side of the trade had barely been known thirty-five years ago. In those earlier times, he stated, every enterprise had two or three apprentices who gave the hats their final luster. Since then it had become impossible to do without a permanent group of workers to finish hats.[19]

Unlike the journeymen who prepared and felted hats, the journeymen who worked on the finishing side were paid by the day. While the long-term effects of the introduction of hare into the trade placed a downward pressure upon the piece rates paid to *fouleurs*, the growing demand for labor on the finishing side of the trade resulted in substantial upward pressure upon the day rates paid to *approprieurs*. Since it was not possible to increase their productivity by technical

19. "Les ouvriers approprieurs ne sont pas de la même importance dans les fabriques que les fouleurs. Ce sont des journaliers qu'on ne connoissoit presque pas il y a 35 ans. Chaque fabrique de chapeaux à Lyon avoit deux ou trois apprentis qui donnoient la lustre aux chapeaux; mais aujourd'hui qu'on a perfectionné tous les arts, on ne peut plus se passer des approprieurs." B.M. Lyon, MS. 114 107, "Lettre de Mr. Buisson à MM. les maîtres-gardes et deputés du corps des maîtres et marchands chapeliers de la ville de Lyon."

means, master hatters sought to bring their output into line with higher rates by changing the form of the wage. Their solution to the relative scarcity of journeymen on the finishing side of the trade was to replace the day rate by a scale of piece rates that required a fuller (or longer) working day to generate an income equivalent to the daily rate. In addition, they tried to increase the number of *approprieurs*. Journeymen working on the finishing side of the trade were therefore faced with attempts to create a new category of workers, known as *alloués* or *dresseurs,* who had not served an apprenticeship in the prescribed manner. In the long term both these developments meant the possibility of reductions in the sums that finishers earned and a substantially more dense and labor-intensive working day.

In practice, there was no automatic or predetermined outcome to any of these possibilities. At one extreme it was possible for journeymen on the felting side of the trade to produce hats made of hare but to earn the rates paid for the manufacture of pure beaver hats, earning as much for three days' work as they had done for a week. At the other it was possible for master hatters to cut rates to levels compatible with new technical and market conditions. Between these two extremes there were many gradations of possibility for maneuver. Much depended upon the identity of the finished product. Hats made mainly from hare, but containing a little beaver fur, could be classed as beaver hats. This, after all, had been what had happened with so-called half-beaver hats, or *demi-castors*. Alternatively, however, such hats could be labeled ordinary hats—*chapeaux communs*—and paid at half the rate. Changes could be made in the shape, size, and content of hats so that established piece rates bore little relation to the article actually produced. On the finishing side of the trade, changes could be made in the form of the wage so that its relation to an established set of working practices was modified irretrievably. Finally, changes could be made in the composition of the workforce so that procedures recognized by particular groups of workers could become anachronistic eccentricities.

At different times and in different places, each of these possibilities arose. The disputes and conflicts between masters and journeymen that they occasioned thus have a very modern appearance. At the same time, however, they were conducted within the terms of reference of the procedures and vocabulary of eighteenth-century France. This meant that they were conducted mainly in the courts and drew upon the language of the law.

There was of course no labor law in eighteenth-century France. Nonetheless, journeymen in the hatting trade made repeated and extensive use of the courts in disputes with their masters. They were able to do so because, for much of the eighteenth century, the civil law in France remained decidedly ambiguous about the legal status of journeymen. Although they had no formal rights within the corporations, journeymen enjoyed a legal status that owed much to the tradition of jurisprudence that ensured that the wages they earned were the price of making a hat. Since they were paid a price for the use of their labor, the wage relation was a contractual relationship of a very much more extensive sort than it was to become in the nineteenth century. It implied a certain recognition of the rights of the producer as well as an obligation to perform such work as had been promised. The recognition that journeymen enjoyed certain distinctive rights as wage earners lay at the core of their repeated recourse to the courts.

An awareness of their rights as producers was not the only significant feature of the culture of journeymen in the hatting trade. Like their masters, they also shared in a situation that, however distinct local conditions may have been, transcended geographical particularities. Their concerns found expression in elaborate and highly extensive networks of migration, correspondence, and cooperation between workers in different localities.

In this, the associations formed by journeymen hatters resembled the best known eighteenth-century journeymen's associations, the *compagnonnages*. Like them, they were geographically extensive, semi-clandestine bodies. Unlike them, their membership was limited to the hatting trade and drew upon categories of worker not usually associated with the *compagnonnages*. A comparison of the two forms of association suggests ways in which it might be possible to divest the history of journeymen's associations in eighteenth-century France of some of its timelessness.[20]

Relations between journeymen hatters and the best known of the *compagnonnages,* the *compagnons du devoir,* were not always easy. The reasons for this tension were closely related to the growing use of hare instead of beaver fur to make hats. Skill in the hatting trade was largely a function of familiarity with the type of material used to make finished articles. As the materials used in the trade became less exotic, the available pool of labor became more substantial. Migrants of different kinds (and, as in many trades, the workforce of the hatting trade contained several types of migrant) became increasingly interchangeable as the materials used in the trade became less diverse. The rights and identities of migrants who had been sent to serve an apprenticeship in one of the principal centers of the trade became less easy to distinguish from those claimed by the itinerant journeymen who also came to work there. As beaver gave way to hare, journeymen who had settled in Paris, Lyon, and Marseille were placed on very much the same footing as their counterparts from hundreds of localities all over provincial France.

The use of hare in the hatting trade appears to have developed first in Marseille during the second quarter of the eighteenth century. In their statutes of 1716, the hatters of Marseille proscribed the production of hats made solely

20. On these associations, see Emile Coornaert, *Les Compagnonnages en France* (Paris, 1966); Cynthia Truant, "Solidarity and Symbolism among Journeymen Artisans: The Case of *Compagnonnage,*" *Comparative Studies in Society and History* 21 (1979): 214–226; Jean Lecuir, "Associations ouvrières de l'époque moderne: Clandestinité et culture populaire," *Revue du Vivarais,* 1979:272–90; Michael Sonenscher, "Mythical Work: The *Compagnonnages* of Eighteenth-Century France," in Patrick Joyce, ed., *The Historical Meanings of Work* (London, 1987); D. Garrioch and M. Sonenscher, "*Compagnonnages,* Confraternities, and Journeymen's Associations in Eighteenth-Century Paris," *European History Quarterly* 16 (1986): 25–45.

from hare or rabbit fur as well as the use of a felting solution.[21] In this, they reproduced the injunctions of the series of royal *arrêts* that had culminated in the *arrêt* of August 1700. By the spring of 1732, however, violations of the prohibition had become so widespread that the corporation decided to take legal action to enforce its statutes.[22] Two dozen hats produced by a manufacturer named Barnabé Carbonnel were confiscated. Carbonnel moved his business to Aix where he had a son and appealed to the Parlement of Provence. The Parlement upheld his appeal and the hatters of Marseille carried the case to the Conseil d'état.

Between 1733 and 1735 both sides produced evidence to support their claims. Carbonnel presented statements from merchants in Montpellier recording their satisfaction with the hats they had bought from him at the Beaucaire fair. A large commercial house in Marseille stated that the hats were extremely popular among its correspondents in Spain. The corporation was, however, able to produce more weighty support. A Haiti merchant reported that the hats were unsalable there. The Chamber of Commerce of Marseille stated that the increased consumption of hare had resulted in a slump in the price of chevron and vicuña pelts imported from the Levant and Spain. Memoranda were also produced from the hatters' corporations of Lyon and Paris and, most conclusively, from the Compagnie des Indes, insisting that the use of hare would inflict damage upon the traffic in beaver pelts and upon markets in Spain and the Indies if the hats in question were passed off as beaver hats.[23] The council accordingly overturned the Parlement's ruling, reaffirmed the terms of

21. B.M. Marseille, 2243, *Statuts . . . des maîtres chapeliers* (article 27); A.N. E 1115ᵃ (34), *arrêt du Conseil* (14 June 1735).

22. A.D. Bouches-du-Rhône, 366E²⁴⁸ (17 April 1732).

23. It insisted "non seulement sur le préjudice que recevroit de cette fabrique le commerce de castor, mais encore sur les conséquences qui résulteroient des envoies que l'on pourroit faire en Espagne et aux Indes des chapeaux en question pour y être vendus comme chapeaux de castor." A.N. E 1115ᵃ (34) (14 June 1735). Carbonnel claimed that he was entitled to make the hats because of an ambiguity in the wording of the statutes (B.M. Marseille, factum 14, "Précis du procez de Bernabé Carbonnel").

the *arrêt* of 1700, prohibited the use of hare in the making of hats, and ordered a fine of 1,000 livres for anyone convicted of the offense. Its judgment was ratified by the corporation in November 1735.

Nevertheless, the practice continued. In September of the same year the problem was raised by the hatters of Lyon. During the past few years, they noted, the hatting trade of Lyon had captured much of the Spanish market from the English. This dominant position was now threatened because of the technique of making hats with the proscribed solution.[24] The corporation had in fact already obtained a ruling from the Consulat of Lyon in 1734 condemning what it termed this "fraudulent technique" (*fausse fabrique*) and had lent its support to the hatters of Marseille in their successful legal action over the issue. It decided, nonetheless, to take further measures by petitioning the Contrôle générale des finances to ban the use of the felting solution altogether. In 1736 the prohibition, together with a fine of 1,000 livres, was incorporated into the new corporate statutes.[25]

Eleven years later, however, the scarcity of beaver produced by the War of the Austrian Succession had taken its toll. The corporation reported that shortages and the rising price of the usual materials had forced a number of masters to have recourse to the special solution, whose effects, it emphasized, were pernicious to the production of good-quality hats and whose use, it claimed, had ruined the hatting trade of Marseille.[26] It called again for enforcement of the prohibition of the solution in making felt from hare fur.

This was to be the last hostile reference to the use of the *eau de composition* by a corporation. Whether or not its use

24. A.D. Rhône, 3E 7879 (266) (19 September 1735).
25. A.D. Rhône, 3E 7880 (258) (7 August 1736).
26. "Plusieurs maîtres ne pouvant employer les matières accoutumées, devenues trop chères depuis plusieurs années, sont obligés pour pouvoir faire bon marché et trouver à vivre, d'employer de mauvaises matières et de se servir de ce que l'on appelle le secret, qui a été reconnu si pernicieux au commerce et à la bonne qualité des chapeaux, et qui a perdu la manufacture de Marseille, autrefois si considérable." A.D. Rhône, 3E 7891 (94) (27 February 1747).

had ruined the trade in Marseille (and subsequent information indicates that it had not), it is clear that the use of the solution there was now widespread and that the hatters' corporation of Marseille had abandoned its previous intransigence. As the manufacturing center that was furthest from Paris and least able to rely upon supplies of beaver pelts from the Compagnie des Indes, it was even more vulnerable than Lyon to war-induced dearths. In 1751 the hatters of Marseille accepted what to them was the inevitable and revoked the deliberation of 1735 that had outlawed the use of the *eau de composition*. The deliberation, they stated, had been made at a time when the solution was little known or understood. Since then, it had become essential to use rabbit and hare fur to make hats, and the solution had been perfected.[27]

Some doubts remained, and in December 1755 it was necessary to repeat the decision to revoke the deliberation of 1735.[28] In 1765 the use of the solution was consecrated by the publication of the abbé Nollet's contribution to the dictionary of the Académie des sciences, *L'Art de faire des chapeaux*, in which details of the preparation were described very fully. By 1777 the practice was so widespread that even in the little town of Chalon-sur-Saône a journeyman could complain when his *chef-d'oeuvre* was rejected by the local corporation because it had been made with the preparation. He argued that the solution was widely used in Lyon and even in Paris. It made it easier to make a hat and the results were of higher quality. All the master hatters in Chalon used the solution, he claimed.[29]

27. "Cette délibération avoit pour objet d'empêcher une nouvelle fabrication qui n'étoit pas encore connue. Mais du depuis on a reconnu par une plus parfaite connoissance de la manière de préparer les poils de lièvre et de lapin, soit par la privation où l'on se trouve depuis longtemps de certaines matières qui étoient employées autrefois à la fabrication des chapeaux, que l'usage des peaux de lapins et de lièvre étoit absolument nécessaire." A.D. Bouches-du-Rhône, 380E[238], fol. 546v (18 May 1751).

28. Ibid., 380E[247], fol. 1161 (10 December 1755).

29. "A Lyon et même à Paris on n'emploie que le poil de lièvre secrété. Que la composition du chapeau en est plus facile et plus belle; que cela est même tellement d'usage que les maîtres chapeliers de cette ville n'en tiennent et n'en vendent pas d'autres." A.C. Chalon-sur-Saône, FF 39 (5 April 1777).

By then the hostility of the corporations had ended. Opposition to the *eau de composition* was now maintained by the journeymen. As a result, both the terms in which that opposition was couched and the manner in which it was organized changed. This, in part, was because the content of the *eau de composition* had changed, as hatters adopted the alarming practice of adding mercury to the solution. More importantly, however, it was because the opposition was now carried by journeymen's associations and inherited the ambiguous social and legal position that they occupied. As this position changed, so too did the character of relations between journeymen and their masters.

7

Journeymen's Confraternities
and the Law

Journeymen's associations in the hatting trade already had a long history by the last quarter of the eighteenth century. In 1756 the journeymen of Paris stated that they had maintained a society for the benefit of their fellows who needed assistance for over three hundred years.[1] The confraternity— named the Confrérie de Saint-Michel, Saint-Jacques, et Saint-Philippe—had been recognized by two papal bulls in 1681 and 1755 and was attached to the church of Sainte-Geneviève des Ardens. It was later transferred to the church of Sainte-Marie-Madeleine on the Ile-de-la-Cité. A second confraternity, named the Confrérie de la Sainte-Vierge et de Saint-François de Sales, was affiliated to the Carmelite abbey on the place Maubert. It too was accorded a papal bull in 1757.[2]

Formal recognition by the Church was complemented by a more limited and ambiguous acknowledgment of the rights of Parisian journeymen by the secular authorities. The existence of the confraternity was approved by La Reynie, the first *lieutenant général de police*, in 1673.[3] The seventeenth-century statutes of the corporation supplied journeymen with a more practical, formal identity, which entitled them to appeal to the courts if it was called into question. Article 18 of the statutes of 1658 gave men who had served an apprenticeship in Paris (and they could, of course, have

---

1. "Depuis plus de trois cent ans ils ont établi entre eux une société pour le soulagement de leurs confrères qui se trouvent avoir besoin de secours." B.N. MS. Joly de Fleury 1590, fol. 175.
2. Ibid., fol. 26 et seq. (1760).
3. Ibid.

been born elsewhere) preferential rights of employment over journeymen from the provinces. In September 1699 the Parisian journeymen began legal proceedings to obtain the enforcement of the article and prevent masters from employing outsiders known as *compagnons battans la semelle* ("shoe bashers").[4] The action was accompanied by meetings and a collection. The corporation responded by claiming (with more than a little exaggeration) that assemblies and seditious gatherings designed to compel masters to employ the men that the journeymen chose were an entirely unprecedented occurrence in the Parisian trades.[5]

They reported that the journeymen met once a month and on the feast days of Saint Michel, Saint Jacques, and Saint Philippe. Members of the association were expected to make a monthly contribution to a *bourse commune*, or common fund. The fund was used, they claimed, to enforce selective boycotts of particular workshops by providing journeymen who refused to work there with sufficient money to enable them to live. As a result, every master hatter had found it impossible to meet orders because of the insufficient number of journeymen.[6] The claim suggests that the trade had been affected by a combination of large-scale

4. B.N. manuscrit français 21 793, fol. 178. In the London hatting trade at the same time, a number of small master hatters or "master workers" were attempting to control the supply of "walkers," journeymen who moved from shop to shop to manufacture hats on a putting-out basis (see Corner, "The London Hatting Trade," cited above, chap. 4, n. 6). The men that the Parisian journeymen objected to were not journeymen of this kind. They were termed, very precisely, "compagnons du dehors, appellez compagnons battans la semelle."

5. "Il est inouy que dans aucun autre corps d'arts et métiers des particuliers se soient avisés de s'attrouper et assembler pour réduire les maistres dudit métier à la nécessité de recevoir parmy eux tels compagnons qu'il leur plaise." B.N. manuscrit français 21 793, fol. 176. In fact, there were disputes in the building trades over exactly the same issue at the same time (see Sonenscher, *Work and Wages*).

6. "Ils se servent de ce fonds pour quand ils veullent rendre tous les ouvroirs vuides et faire sortir tous les compagnons qui sont de leurs caballes, de telle manière que quand il leur plaise tous les maistres demeurent dans l'impossibilité de pouvoir faire les ouvrages qu'ils ont entrepris faute de compagnon." B.N. manuscrit français 21 793, fol. 176.

orders, possibly associated with military contracts arising from the war of the League of Augsburg, and short-term labor scarcity. The corporation called for the prohibition of the confraternity and freedom to employ *compagnons battans la semelle.*

The decision of the Chambre de police of the Châtelet—the court that dealt in the first instance with disputes in the Parisian corporations—early in 1700 maintained the substance of the journeymen's formal identity. Although assemblies under the mantle of a confraternity (or otherwise) were prohibited and journeymen were prevented from placing one another in work, the court ordered masters to give preference to *compagnons de Paris* provided that they did not demand higher wages than journeymen from the provinces. It also restricted the number of apprentices allowed to each master to one and forbade the employment of workers known as *alloués,* who had served no apprenticeship and were therefore precluded from access to the *maîtrise.*[7]

The two issues at the heart of this dispute—the employment of "foreigners" (*étrangers*) and the question of *alloués*—arose again in 1721 in a conflict that was largely the result of the inflation that had occurred during Law's financial experiment. Journeymen working on the felting side of the trade had obtained higher piece rates (an additional 5 sous on each type of hat), the first increase, one of them said, for over twenty years.[8] Once monetary stability had been restored, some masters appear to have decided to reestablish the old rates. Early in the year a hatter named Lacauche announced his decision to do so to his workers and was promptly victimized. The journeymen he employed either left spontaneously without giving the statutory period of a month's notice or were forced to do so by their comrades.

---

7. "Pourvu qu'ils ne veulent exiger des maîtres un plus grand salaire que les compagnons etrangers." Archives de la Préfecture de police, Fonds Lamoignon 20, fol. 65 (20 January 1700). See also B.N. F 26429, *Recueil de statuts, ordonnances, et règlements de la communauté des maîtres et marchands chapeliers* (Paris, 1775), 40 (27 February 1700).

8. A.N. Y 14 932 (10 and 13 November 1721).

One of them later stated that he had been warned by the others that, unless he walked out, he would be forced to eat grass and would never find work in Paris again.[9] Journeymen who had walked out of their shops were paid 6 livres 10 sous a week by the confraternity until they were placed elsewhere.

The scale of the disruption prompted the corporation to establish a system of *billets de congé* in July 1721. Under this procedure journeymen were expected to present a printed certificate issued by the corporation that testified to their good conduct and the satisfactory completion of their work before they could be taken on elsewhere. The formality was one that journeymen particularly resented as a substantial violation of their natural right to dispose of their labor as they chose.[10] It was clearly designed to prevent the journeymen's confraternity from controlling the supply of labor.

There are many indications that this control had been effective. The confraternity could pay out-of-work journeymen an amount that was sufficient for daily subsistence over a long period, in order to deprive individual employers of an adequate workforce. As a result, the campaign of selective victimization lasted for nearly a year. Journeymen who were reluctant to leave their employers were warned that their names would be struck from the confraternity's list of members and that they would no longer be entitled to any of its ordinary benefits for illness or accidents. Attempts to replace Parisian journeymen by men from outside the capital appear to have been a failure. One of the men involved in the dispute, when asked to explain the journeymen's hostility to workers from the provinces, denied that it existed. He explained that in all the five years that he had worked as a journeyman he had never seen a Parisian journeyman deny employment to anyone from the provinces. This, he added

9. "Ils luy feroient manger de l'herbe et qu'il pourroit compter qu'il ne travailleroit plus à Paris." Ibid., deposition of Jacques Langlois.
10. See above, chapter 1. Litigation over the question was a frequent occurrence in many other trades (see Sonenscher, *Work and Wages*).

artlessly, was because there were no journeymen from the provinces employed by Parisian master hatters.[11]

The duration of the dispute is indicative of the resources of the confraternity. One of the journeymen who gave evidence in the subsequent legal proceedings described what (despite the prohibition of 1700) was clearly a well-established mutual aid society. Each journeyman contributed 4 sous a week and could expect to receive 5 livres a week if ill or otherwise unable to work. The confraternity had several treasurers who collected weekly contributions from journeymen in each hatting enterprise and met on every second Sunday of the month at the church of Sainte-Geneviève des Ardens. During the dispute there were also regular meetings at the church of Saint-Denis de la Chartre and, more informally, in an inn called the Saint-François on the place Maubert. They were open to anyone engaged in journey work, even masters without their own shops. One of the confraternity's treasurers was indeed a master working as a journeyman.[12]

The presence of master hatters within the journeymen's confraternity is not particularly surprising. Nor, in the first half of the eighteenth century, was it a peculiarity of the hatting trade in Paris. Journeymen's confraternities in Lyon and Marseille also included several master hatters among their members. In every locality the relatively wide gulf between the core of the trade, where most journeymen worked, and the periphery of very much smaller enterprises, where wage labor was virtually nonexistent, meant that in reality the formal division between masters and journeymen was very much more fluid. Journeymen who repaired and sold hats—or took on subcontracted work—were unlikely to be prosecuted. There were also master hatters who worked for wages. Some three-quarters of the membership of the Pari-

---

11. "Depuis environ cinq ans qu'il est compagnon dudit métier de chapelier il n'a jamais vu que les compagnons de Paris . . . ayent empêchés les compagnons de province de travailler chez les maîtres chapeliers de Paris puisqu'il n'y a point de maîtres qui n'en ait." A.N. Y 14 932 (10 and 13 November 1721).

12. Ibid.

sian hatters' corporation consisted of masters who did not manufacture hats.[13] It is likely that some of them worked for wages at times or took on subcontracted work for the larger enterprises. The former activity was acceptable to journeymen, the latter was not. The journeymen objected when smaller masters took on unapprenticed workers, or *alloués*, for the benefit of employers in the larger enterprises. This issue was to occasion a long dispute in Lyon a generation later.[14] As a result, the position of master hatters within journeymen's confraternities became increasingly uncomfortable, while the formal status and public identity of the confraternities themselves became a matter of sharper debate.

Further light was thrown upon the Parisian confraternity during another dispute in 1725 and 1726. In June 1725 the hatters' corporation drew up a scale of piece rates fixing the *tarif* on the felting side of the trade as follows:

beaver hats (7–9 oz.)	30 sous
beaver hats (9–12 oz.)	35 sous
half-beaver (*demi-castor*)	22 sous
vicuña (*vigogne*)	20 sous

The journeymen appealed against the new scale of piece rates, but their action was unsuccessful.[15] The Chambre de police reiterated its condemnation of the confraternity and ordered the confiscation of its papers.

The rules contained in the papers were relatively elaborate and suggest that the association's membership was somewhat different in composition from the peripatetic *compagnons battans la semelle*, to whom the journeymen had objected in 1699 and 1721. The association was open to anyone aged forty or under who was working as a journeyman in the trade. Members were entitled to 5 livres a week for up to

13. See above, chapter 5.
14. See below, pp. 90–91.
15. A.N. Y 9498 (30 August 1726); B.N. F 26429 (6 September 1726); Archives de la Préfecture de police, Fonds Lamoignon 28, fol. 633.

six months for illness or injury and a further 6 livres a month during any subsequent period of convalescence. The aged or infirm (who joined the confraternity before their fortieth birthday) were entitled to a monthly allowance of 4 livres. The *bourse* was maintained by weekly contributions, and the rules stipulated that anyone who refused to make a collection (*qui refuse à quester*) would be struck off the list of members. There were four treasurers (*boursiers*) elected in alternating pairs at six-month intervals. The confraternity was, in other words, a well-established institution whose existence was well known to most master hatters and, in normal circumstances, was probably accepted by the corporation.[16]

Despite the condemnation by the Chambre de police in 1726, an inquiry into confraternities mounted by the Parlement of Paris in 1760 revealed that the association was still intact.[17] Its continued survival was a reflection not only of journeymen's abiding concerns but also of the ambiguity of the law during the first half of the eighteenth century. Although the courts repeatedly prohibited assemblies under the guise of a confraternity or otherwise (*sous prétexte de confrérie ou autrement*), the wording of successive rulings left room for a range of possible constructions to be placed upon their implications. The confraternity itself was not specifically named in a judicial ruling until 1726. The term "assembly" also lent itself to discretionary interpretation, and it is not clear whether it referred to attendance at mass or the collection of money by individuals for the confraternity. The characteristic imprecision of the courts' rulings ensured that the association was able to survive within the discretionary netherworld of arbitrary authority.

When the courts did act they did so only in response to pressure from the hatters' corporation and were relatively circumspect in meeting the claims that the masters placed before them. They upheld the journeymen's claim to enjoy a special status as against those who had served an appren-

---

16. A.N. Y 14 938 (17 March 1726).
17. B.N. MS. Joly de Fleury 1590, fol. 26 et seq.

ticeship outside Paris. Nor did they prevent journeymen
from initiating collective legal proceedings, as they did in
1699 and 1725. This de facto recognition of collective association may at first seem surprising, but there was nothing in
the law that distinguished legal proceedings mounted by
journeymen in the trades from proceedings collectively initiated by the inhabitants of a village or a suburb. Journeymen
hatters were not, it was true, a corporation; but neither were
many other groups of people who presented their claims
against local landowners or other seigneurial or corporate
bodies. Since civil rights were titles of possession of an exceptional kind, anyone named in the wording of those titles
(like journeymen, who were named in the relevant articles
of the statutes of their masters' corporation) could challenge
modifications to their provisions. The generic term *coalition*,
which was to underpin revolutionary and postrevolutionary
legislation on combinations in the trades, did not exist in the
first half of the eighteenth century. The meaning of the term
cabale was very much less precise. It was used by the duc de
Saint-Simon to describe intrigues by members of the court of
Louis XIV as well as by master artisans in disputes over the
management of corporate affairs. Journeymen who combined to use the courts could and did claim that their actions
were of a different order.[18]

In these circumstances, recourse to the courts and familiarity with the procedures of litigation were by no means

18. The word *coalition* appears in Le Chapelier's report on behalf of the
comité de constitution to the National Assembly introducing the law of 14
June 1791 that bears his name, but not in the wording of the law itself: J. M.
Thompson, ed., *French Revolution Documents* (London, 1948), 82–86. The
term *cabale* was widely used in eighteenth-century civil regulation affecting
the trades and in many other contexts too: see Emmanuel Le Roy Ladurie,
"Le Système de la cour (Versailles vers 1709)," *L'Arc* 65 (1979): 21–35;
"Auprès du roi: La Cour," *Annales, E.S.C.* (1983): 21–41. For a pioneering
discussion of the formal status of journeymen, see Steven L. Kaplan,
"Réflexions sur la police du monde de travail, 1700–1791," *Revue historique*
529 (1979): 17–77. Kaplan's characterization of the relationship between
journeymen and the law does not address the more active part played by
journeymen in eighteenth-century litigation. The question is discussed at
greater length in Sonenscher, *Work and Wages.*

limited to master artisans. The law, moreover, was part of the texture of work. The provisions of corporate statutes affected the composition of the workforce. Royal *arrêts* affected the nature of the materials used in production. Finally, after 1725 the rates paid to journeymen on the felting side of the Parisian trade were also set by the courts. The law provided a more extensive definition of relations of production than a simple ascription of rights to ownership of materials and finished products. Its terms and propositions formed a part of the structure of everyday transactions in the trade.

The ambiguity of the law and its relation to the situation of journeymen was more pronounced in Lyon and even more so in Marseille. The revised statutes of the hatters' corporation in Lyon, which were drawn up in 1736, provided journeymen with the right to belong to the masters' confraternity on payment of the modest annual fee of 15 sous.[19] It is likely that this opportunity was not entirely to the journeymen's own taste. An attempt to collect the fee in 1741 resulted in a brawl when over a dozen journeymen employed by a hatter named Derussy refused to pay, on the grounds that, as one of them said, it was against the rules (*contre la règle et l'usage*).[20]

The existence of an independent journeymen's association can be assumed. Its identity is clear from an undated set of rules entitled "Règles des compagnons chapeliers de la bourse de Lyon," contained among the papers of a journeyman who died in the Hôtel Dieu toward 1753.[21] The rules were similar to those of the Parisian journeymen's association. There was an initial membership fee of 4 livres 4 sous and fortnightly contributions of 4 sous by everyone in work. Payments to the ill or infirm were fixed at the smaller amount of 4 livres a week for up to four months. Everyone, whether in or out of work, was required to contribute 2 sous

19. A.D. Rhône, 3E 7080 (258) (7 August 1736).
20. A.D. Rhône, BP 3126 (12 July 1741).
21. Archives de l'Hôtel Dieu, Lyon, G 88, papers of Antoine Barbaroux.

to the costs of funerals and to attend the service. Article 15 of the rules allowed for additional collections if exceptional circumstances meant that ordinary revenue was insufficient. Events in the trade at the time indicate what such circumstances might have been.

The confraternity was formally recognized by the Consulat of Lyon in May 1744 in the aftermath of a substantial revolt by silk weavers in that year. It very rapidly became the object of a hostile campaign by the master hatters, who claimed that the journeymen had taken advantage of the weakness of the authorities to obtain legal recognition for their association. Like the hatters of Paris a generation earlier, they stated that it had been used to deny work to journeymen from outside the city and was directed, in particular, at a new category of workers in the trade, known here as *affermés*.

Like the Parisian *alloués*, *affermés* were unapprenticed casual laborers taken on as felters by small masters on the periphery of the trade working on the account of more substantial manufacturers. Their appearance was designed to overcome restrictions on the number of apprentices allowed to each master and to circumvent journeymen's own working arrangements. It was intended that they should be taken on for six months and instructed in the art of felting by established journeymen. After this period they were to be entitled to undertake journey work themselves. The journeymen were less than enthusiastic about the proposal and suggested a period of initiation of three years rather than six months. They also walked out of workshops where *affermés* were employed and on one occasion assaulted both a master and the *affermé* he had engaged. Eventually the Consulat was forced to intervene, and in December 1746 it issued an ordinance banning the confraternity but increasing the period of initiation required of *affermés* to a year.[22]

---

22. A.C. Lyon, HH 32, "Mémoire des marchands chapeliers," [1746]; "Mémoire des marchands fabricants de Lyon," [1746]; *ordonnance du Consulat*, 20 February 1746. These events coincided with a protracted dispute

It was doubtless because of their anxieties about the continued existence of the confraternity that the hatters pressed the Consulat to publish the royal letters patent of 2 January 1749 prohibiting combinations among workers. Its provisions, they stated, would be useful in the management of every type of manufactory, and especially in the hatting trade.[23] A year later, however, they complained that the letters patent had been widely ignored, particularly by journeymen claiming to be new arrivals to Lyon and by women workers who—in keeping with the limited and exceptional character of civil obligation—argued that the ruling did not apply to them at all. Accordingly, the corporation decided to set up a system of registration that would apply to everyone in the trade, so that no one would be able to walk out on work until it had been completed.[24]

It is possible, although there is no direct evidence of the fact, that the letters patent of 2 January 1749 were precipitated by disputes in the hatting trade. The tension in Lyon was matched by more open conflict in Paris and Marseille.[25] Conditions in all three centers were undoubtedly affected by the end of the War of the Austrian Succession, the revival of production, and the greater opportunities available for journeymen to move from *fabrique* to *fabrique* in pursuit of better earnings. One indication of the upward pressure upon wage rates can be found in a widespread stoppage in Paris that began in the summer of 1748 when a number of journeymen working on the rue Saint-Sauveur walked out after they had

---

within the hatters' corporation itself over the administration of its financial affairs. There is no evidence, however, that the two disputes were linked, although it is difficult to believe that there were no connections. On the dispute within the corporation, see A.N. X^{1b} 3572 (7 October 1747); 3584 (31 August 1748); 3614 (24 October 1750); 3618 (11 January 1751); 7879 (11 December 1743); 7961 (21 August 1748); 7998 (28 November 1748).

23. A.D. Rhône, 3E 9686 (286) (15 September 1749). The text of the letters patent is published in Emile Levasseur, *Histoire des classes ouvrières et de l'industrie en France avant 1789* (Paris, 1901), 510–11.

24. A.D. Rhône, 3E 9681 (265) (11 August 1750).

25. There was also a stoppage in Rouen: see A.D. Seine-Maritime, 5E 207 (17 June 1750).

been refused an advance of the relatively considerable sum of 100 livres each on their wages. The conflict also drew in journeymen who dyed hats, forcing the corporation to obtain a ruling from the Parlement of Paris in July 1748 that fixed the length of their working day (from 5 A.M. to 9 P.M., including two hours for meals) and set the daily rate paid to dyers and journeymen working on the finishing side of the trade (*approprieurs*) at 40 sous, which, it stated, had been the practice for a long time.[26]

The dispute lasted for several months. Toward the end of September 1748, nine journeymen were arrested and imprisoned in the Conciergerie.[27] They appealed to the Parlement and were released after a week. Litigation between the journeymen and the corporation continued during the winter of that year. Three dozen master hatters intervened in the proceedings to bring a separate action in opposition to the regulations of July 1748. The Parlement dismissed both appeals and in March 1749 ordered the implementation of the two police sentences of 1700 and 1726 that respectively limited journeymen's rights to assemble and defined the scale of piece rates paid to workers in the trade.[28]

The issue of piece rates remained a source of contention. In 1751 there was a further dispute over the rates paid to journeymen on the felting side of the trade for making beaver hats with ostrich feathers, known as *castors à plumets*. The journeymen claimed that they contained more beaver fur than other types of hat and, because of the additional time needed to prepare the felt, refused to make the hats for less than 5 livres each. The corporation again had recourse to the Parlement, which ratified its recommendation for a rate of 4 livres for *castors à plumets* and 3 livres for *demi-castors à plu-*

26. A.N. X^{1b} 3582 (31 July 1748); Archives de la Préfecture de police, Fonds Lamoignon 38, fol. 436 (31 July 1748); B.N. F 26429, p. 150.

27. Archives de la Préfecture de police, Ab 108 (29 September 1748).

28. A.N. X^{1a} 4044, fol. 223 (3 October 1748); X^{1a} 7640, fol. 118v (5 October 1748); X^{1a} 4045, fols. 58, 165v (26 November 1748 and 4 December 1748); X^{1a} 4045, fol. 132v (2 December 1748); X^{1a} 7649, fol. 188v (15 March 1749).

mets. These rates, the hatters insisted, were fair because they would mean that a worker could earn up to 32 livres a week.[29]

The claim introduced what was to become one of the principal sources of conflict in the trade during the second half of the century: the amount of work that a hatter could do in a day. It echoed a dispute over exactly the same issue that was in progress in Marseille. There, however, the question was inextricably bound up with the uncertain legal status and rights of journeymen in the trade.

In March 1750 an assembly of sixty journeymen hatters representing the generality of those working in the trade of Marseille (*la généralité des compagnons chapeliers*) decided to take legal action against the corporation because some masters were requiring journeymen to make three hats a day. There were, they stated, some workers prepared to make that number in return for a "modest" increase in their wages. The practice, they noted, had had two deleterious consequences. The first was the violation of established rules. The second was the effect of higher productivity upon employment. A number of journeymen were out of work. Yet if each individual made no more than two hats a day, the journeymen claimed, there would be sufficient work for everyone in the trade.[30]

The rules in question had in fact been inserted as article 30 of the statutes of the master hatters' corporation in 1716.[31] Soon after the ratification of the statutes by the Parlement of Provence, the journeymen's association embarked upon legal action to enforce the article. In 1719 its priors (*prieurs*)

29. "Un ouvrier peut gagner jusqu'à trente deux livres par semaine." Archives de la Préfecture de police, Fonds Lamoignon 40 (24 March 1751).

30. "Il est divers ouvriers qui font tous les jours d'oeuvre trois chapeaux sollicités par les maîtres qui leur y portent en augmentant leurs salaires ou journée de quelque modique retribution." Its consequences were as follows: "Le premier de tous est l'infraction aux règlements; le second est que cela contribue aussy à faire trouver beaucoup d'ouvriers sur le pavé, qui trouveroit tous de l'ouvrage si chaque ouvrier ne faisoit que deux chapeaux par jour, ce qui est ce qu'il doit faire selon la règle." A.D. Bouches-du-Rhône, 367E²³⁹, fol. 203v (8 March 1750).

31. B.M. Marseille, 2243.

and *syndics* demanded that every master and journeyman should be prohibited from making more than two hats a day, since it was "morally impossible" for anyone to make more and produce finished work of good quality.[32] The action was successful and the norm of two hats a day remained in force throughout the first half of the century. It was retained as article 38 of the revised statutes of the hatters' corporation of 1746. In March 1749 two masters were fined by the corporation for violating the article.[33]

The journeymen's success was partly a result of the considerable legal rights they enjoyed. The incorporation of the trades was much more recent in cities in the south of France than it had been in Paris and the towns of the north.[34] In Lyon the trade was incorporated in 1686; in Marseille in 1716. In the latter city, the corporation was grafted on to an already existent confraternity in which journeymen occupied an established place. This confraternity, named the Confrérie de la Luminaire de Sainte-Catherine de Sienne, was not restricted to members of the hatting trade. In the seventeenth century and until some time during the third decade of the eighteenth, it was composed of masters and journeymen drawn from the hosiery, hatting, and cloth-finishing trades (*bonnetiers, chapeliers, tondeurs, fouleurs, teinturiers,* and *facturiers en draps*).

In 1715 its ceremonial life was affected by a dispute between masters and journeymen in the hatting trade. The masters refused to allow journeymen to take part in the confraternity's torchlit procession of the Holy Sacrament and, in the following year, proceeded to elect its priors without the journeymen. The journeymen appealed to the Parlement. Since time immemorial, they complained, journeymen in the hosiery, cloth-factoring, and hatting trades had assembled to

32. "Inhibition et déffenses seront faites auxdits maistres et compagnons de fabriquer plus de deux chapeaux par jour moyennant qu'ils soient ouvrés entiers, poncés et pincetez—étant moralement impossible qu'ils puissent en faire davantage et qu'ils soient bien travaillez et en bon état." A.D. Bouches-du-Rhône, 364E^{350} (30 March 1719).

33. Ibid., 380E^{234}, fol. 243 (20 March 1749).

34. See Maurice Agulhon, *Pénitents et francs-maçons de l'ancienne Provence* (Paris, 1969).

elect two priors on the same day that their masters elected their own four priors. The threat of protracted litigation appears to have encouraged the masters to seek a settlement. Before the Parlement was able to produce a verdict, the two sides came to an accommodation. Its terms ensured that the journeymen's rights were fully recognized. Their two priors were to continue to be elected every Thursday before Shrove Tuesday and their place in the mass and torchlit processions held on the feast days of Sainte Catherine de Sienne, Christmas, and Twelfth Night was to be respected. The journeymen were also to continue to enjoy the right to use the confraternity's torches in funeral processions for deceased members, their wives, or children, and, in general, to enjoy all the rights to which they had been entitled in the past.[35] The agreement was duly ratified by both the masters and the journeymen. At the same time, an assembly of 142 journeymen hatters gave its approval to the corporation's statutes.[36]

Thus, for much of the first half of the eighteenth century, the situation of journeymen in the three cities was at once distinct—insofar as each group could look to the courts for recognition of certain particular rights—and subject to forms of public acknowledgment of a similar kind. Journeymen who had served an apprenticeship and were settled in one of the three cities were endowed with a certain formal identity and a capacity to claim rights of various kinds. Their formal rights were most extensive in Marseille, where the tradition of Roman law and the status of written contractual undertakings were most pronounced.[37] There, they were

35. "De tous temps et hors de mémoire d'homme, à mezure que les maîtres bonnetiers, facturiers à draps et chapelliers avoint fait leurs quatre prieurs le jour du Jeudy Gras, les compagnons des trois arts s'assembloint au mesme endroit et fesoint deux prieurs d'entre eux, y en ayant mesme eleu pluzieurs qui ont esté prieurs des compagnons et qui l'ont été ensuitte des maîtres." A.D. Bouches-du-Rhône, 366E[240] (1 December 1717).

36. A.D. Bouches-du-Rhône, 366E[241] (24 February 1718); 364E[349] (13 November 1717).

37. The practice of limiting production to two hats a day was written into the statutes of the hatters' corporation of Marseille but does not appear in those of the corporations of Paris or Lyon, which fell within the jurisdiction of the Parlement of Paris. The statutes of the corporation of Marseille of

able not only to invoke statutory authority to regulate their working day (and, like journeymen in Lyon and Paris, the number of apprentices to which each master was entitled), but they were also in possession of an established place within the trade's confraternity. In 1730, when the master hosiers, cloth factors, croppers, fullers, and dyers decided to withdraw from it to form their own separate confraternities, the master hatters invoked their journeyman's rights to prevent them. Since journeymen and workers were part of the confraternity, they argued, their consent was needed before anyone could withdraw.[38]

By 1789 this kind of recognition was a thing of the past. The master hatters, along with masters of the other trades, had withdrawn from the Confrérie de Sainte-Catherine de Sienne, which had become an illegal association of journeymen hatters. It was now described simply as a former charitable foundation (*une ancienne oeuvre pie*) that had become the source of the worst kind of abuses and had come to be equated with the *compagnonnages* in the eyes of the authorities.[39] As the law changed and the nexus of work and legal recognition was progressively dissolved, the forms of journeymen's associations lost something of their particularity. Both the vocabulary of litigation and the language of formal transactions became more resonant of circumstances in the trade as a whole. An increasing synchrony came to inform the dialogue between journeymen and their masters in the three cities as conditions in the trade came to be governed by increasingly similar pressures and concerns.

1716 were modeled explicitly on those of the Parisian corporation but, because of the slightly different legal traditions of the two Parlements, went into greater detail on working arrangements. On the durability of the practice of making no more than two hats in Paris, see below, chapter 12.

38. "Les compagnons et ouvriers étant unis à la confrérie, il faut par un préalable avoir un consentement général desdits compagnons et ouvriers." Ibid., 366E[247] (16 February 1730).

39. E. Isnard, "Documents inédits sur l'histoire du compagnonnage à Marseille au XVIIIe siècle," in J. Hayem, ed., *Mémoires et documents pour servir à l'histoire économique de la Révolution française* 4 (1916): 185–211 (especially 208).

8

Piece Rates and the Content of a Hat

The Seven Years' War and the loss of Canada marked a turning point in the history of the trade. They resulted in a severe shortage of feltable fur whose effects were most acute in Lyon and Marseille. In July 1760 the hatters of Lyon decided to revise their statutes to prevent the loss or theft of the scarce material. In the future, no one was allowed to purchase any fur or damaged hats without knowledge of their provenance. Workers were required to have booklets in which the materials given out to them were recorded and to mark each hat they made with their initials. The penalty for illegally selling fur was a fine of 200 livres, while purchasers of stolen fur faced the draconian penalty of a 1,500-livre fine.[1]

The measures were directed at a practice that was usually tolerated when supplies were adequate. Journeymen hatters were customarily allowed or, in unfavorable circumstances, forced (since the value of damaged goods was not covered by the piece rate) to keep and sell damaged hats. The usage concerned journeymen alone; a sentence following the conviction of an apprentice for selling a hat in 1765 made it clear that it was not customary to credit damaged hats to an apprentice's account.[2] The practice had its advantages for masters, either

1. A.D. Rhône, 3E 9699 (466) (31 July 1760). Similar measures had been taken during the shortage of 1739: A.D. Rhône, 3E 7883 (365) (12 October 1739).
2. "Il n'est pas d'usage de les luy laisser pour son compte, ce qui ne se pratique qu'à l'égard des compagnons." A.D. Rhône, BP 3316 (12 August 1765). According to the master hatter Jacques Buisson, writing in 1781, "toutes les fois qu'un chapeau est gâté par ceux-ci [i.e., the journeymen] dans la fabrication, on le leur laisse, et ils sont forcés de le vendre. Si les ouvriers sont mal-honnêtes, ils s'autorisent de ce qu'ils peuvent vendre

because it allowed them to offer some additional mark of recognition to their journeymen or because it enabled them to circumvent shortages of cash during periods when the trade was slack. Masters and journeymen had somewhat contradictory attitudes to payment in kind: to the former they could represent a convenient substitute for cash or mean the loss of a valuable material; to the latter they could represent a valuable addition to the wage or mean prolonged periods without real money. When the trade was slack the negative attitudes came to the fore on both sides. The theft of materials became a more urgent matter to masters, while journeymen faced their own difficulties in finding purchasers for damaged articles that they had been given in place of wages by financially straitened employers. The result, in the eyes of both parties, was a heightened pressure upon the money wage. This is what occurred almost simultaneously in Lyon and Marseille.

The dispute in Lyon began in 1760 with a demand by journeymen working on the felting side of the trade for higher rates. The demand was the result of a shift away from the production of high-quality beaver hats to hats made of other, cheaper furs. According to the masters, the cheaper hats were quicker to prepare, so that journeymen could earn as much by making more hats a week even if the rates were lower. The *fouleurs* maintained that it was impossible to produce more than nine hats a week; the corporation claimed that they could make a dozen. The journeymen argued that this claim was designed to conceal a maneuver to cut wages. They maintained that it was always possible to rename a hat and pay an individual at a rate appropriate to the cheaper article even though the same amount of time was needed to do the work. The problem was, of course, that when the price of materials increased, the pressure to find some compensation for this relatively fixed medium-term cost by some reduction in short-term costs was considerable. Not only did this situation lead to disputes over the rates paid for hats made of

---

leurs chapeaux défectueux, et, en en gâtant, les vendre [*sic*] avec ceux qu'ils voleront." B.M. Lyon, MS. 114 107.

different materials, it also resulted in delays in the payment of wages themselves. For over a decade, the hatting trade in Lyon was wracked by conflict over the definitions of different types of hat. The journeymen maintained that hats containing some beaver fur should be paid at the rates obtaining for beaver hats; the manufacturers claimed that the amount of beaver fur used in certain types of hat was so negligible (and the time needed to produce them so much less) that the rates should accordingly be lower.

In February 1761 the Consulat of Lyon issued an ordinance setting the rates for four different kinds of hat, running from 50 sous for beaver hats with ostrich feathers (*castors à plumets*) to 15 sous for hats made from vicuña. It also set the daily rate paid to dyers and finishers at 35 sous or 3 livres for working on into the night. The hatters' corporation refused to accept these rates, claiming that they bore no relation to the kinds of hat made in Lyon, and appealed to the Parlement of Paris. Over two hundred journeymen working in Lyon combined to oppose the appeal. They demanded that the rates paid in Lyon be the same as those set for the trade in Paris in 1726 and 1751.[3] They also argued that the ordinance confused a number of different types of hat and made no allowance for the different periods of time needed to make them.

In September the Parlement produced its judgment. It overturned the ordinance of February 1761 and fixed the rates as follows:

beaver hats with feathers	3 livres	
half-beaver hats with feathers	2 livres	10 sous
ordinary beaver hats (9–12 oz.)	1 livre	10 sous
ordinary beaver hats (7–9 oz.)	1 livre	8 sous
half-beavers, or *marcassins*	1 livre	
vicuñas or common hats		15 sous

An extra 3 sous was to be paid if hats contained a modicum of beaver fur for decoration (*dorure*). The rates paid to dyers

3. A.N. X^{1a} 8187 (20 May 1761). On the rates in question, see above, chapter 7.

and finishers were reduced to 30 sous a day, although the rate for work at night remained at 3 livres.[4]

The clarity of the scale was highly misleading. The ruling did not specify the content of the different types of hats it listed, nor did it define what a day's work was. In the prevailing conditions of continuing shortages—especially of beaver fur—and rising orders as the end of the war approached, the ambiguity was an invitation to further conflict.

The conflict came to a head over the definition of beaver, half-beaver, and vicuña hats. In January 1762 the journeymen's two delegates, Chabanon and Deloeuvre, had a summons served upon the firm of Chabert, Maurier et Cie for failing to pay the rates set by the Parlement. They claimed that the firm was paying half-beaver hats at the rate set for vicuñas or *chapeaux communs*. The problem, the journeymen stated, would be resolved once the court was aware of what master hatters were doing. They argued that hats containing beaver and other materials should not be passed off as vicuña hats because they were as time-consuming to make and were sold at the same price as the more highly paid article.[5] The journeymen insisted that the hats they were producing should be paid at the rates of 20 sous (for *demi-castors*) or 28 to 33 sous (for *castors*), rather than the 15 or 23 sous the manufacturers were prepared to pay.[6]

By late January 1762 there was a general cessation of production. According to the masters, the journeymen were concerned with more than just rates. They had demanded an hour for their meals instead of the usual half hour and had insisted upon rates of 20 to 24 sous for making vicuña

4. A.C. Lyon, HH 32, *arrêt* (5 September 1761).

5. "Cette difficulté sera bientôt levée lorsque la Cour sçaura qu'il plaît aux maîtres chapeliers de Lyon d'appeller vigognes des chapeaux qui n'en est [sic] pas, dans lequel au contraire il entre du castor et plusieurs autres sortes de marchandises; qu'il faut autant de tems pour les fabriquer que pour les demy-castors ou marquassins, et que les maîtres les vendent au même prix que les demy-castors ou marcassins." A.D. Rhône, 3E 9702 (28) (20 January 1762); A.N. X^{1a} 7950, fol. 456 (29 April 1762); 7952, fol. 105 (12 May 1762).

6. A.D. Rhône, 3E 3440 (9 January 1762).

hats.[7] The stoppages lasted for several weeks. Although work had resumed by early May, the corporation complained that the journeymen were continuing to collect money to pay for their appeal to the Parlement of Paris.[8] In July the journeymen obtained an *arrêt* that, to the evident horror of the masters, appeared to define half-beaver as beaver hats. Again the firm of Chabert, Maurier et Cie was at the center of the dispute. It later stated that, in order to avoid a stoppage at a time when it was heavily burdened with orders, it had decided to capitulate to the journeymen's demands. A second manufacturer, François Récamier, did the same.[9]

The Parlement of Paris produced a second ruling on the dispute in September 1762. It confirmed the rates set a year earlier but raised the rate for vicuñas or *chapeaux communs* from 15 to 18 sous. It also introduced a new rate of 27 sous for what were termed three-quarter beaver hats.[10] This appears to have ended the dispute. The *arrêt* continued, however, to evade the fundamental problem of the uncertain relationship between the content of hats and the rates at which they were to be paid.

Like the dispute in Lyon, the conflict in Marseille centered upon the rates paid to felters. It too involved long-drawn-out legal proceedings, in the course of which the journeymen of Marseille invoked in support of their own claims the rates that had been set by the Parlement of Paris for the trade in Lyon. The first maneuvers began, however, in April 1761 when the journeymen began legal proceedings

---

7. "Lesdits compagnons . . . veulent que les maîtres leur payent la façon du chapeau de vigogne depuis vingt sols jusques à vingt quatre. . . . Quelques uns voulant qu'on leur donne une heure pour chaque repas quoiqu'ils ne doivent prendre qu'une demi-heure. . . . La pluspart même ont entièrement quitté l'ouvrage et déserté les fabriques, formant des cabales, courant de boutique en boutique pour empêcher le petit nombre de leurs confrères qui conformoit à l'arrest de travailler." Ibid., 3E 9702 (30) (21 January 1762).

8. Ibid., 3E 9702 (229) (3 May 1762); A.N. X^{1a} 4407, fol. 91 (14 July 1762).

9. Ibid., 3E 9703 (390 and 391) (23 and 24 July 1762).

10. A.C. Lyon, HH 32 (1 September 1762).

in Aix to prevent manufacturers from paying them in kind or imposing fines for work that they decided was faulty. The corporation was forced to issue an instruction to its members prohibiting them from paying wages in kind (whether in the form of materials or hats) and from imposing fines under any pretext.[11]

The successful action had been mounted by the journeymen's confraternity, which began making preparations for a more substantial campaign. The weekly contribution of 1 sou levied upon each journeyman was raised to 3 sous, and two extra collectors were elected to manage the fund. In June lists of the journeymen employed in all the *fabriques* of the city were drawn up, and a series of selective stoppages began. The first victims were two brothers, Joseph and Henri Chabaud, whose workshop was deserted in early July. Joseph Chabaud later testified that the brothers had offered to increase their rates but were told by their journeymen that they would not stay at work even if they were paid an écu a hat, because they had no desire to have their arms and legs broken.[12] One of the journeymen was reported to have said that unless their wages were increased they would be forced to work as laborers or find work on the land.[13]

By early August at least four masters had given way and raised their rates. The corporation decided to take action and appealed to the municipal authorities to intervene.[14] On 16 August a dozen journeymen were arrested, the papers of

---

11. A.D. Bouches-du-Rhône, 367E²⁵², fol. 415 (7 May 1761).

12. "Que s'ils leur donneroient un écu ils ne resteroient pas dans leur fabrique parce qu'ils ne vouloient pas se faire rompre les bras et les jambes." A.C. Marseille, FF 370.

13. "Que si les maîtres ne leur augmentoient leurs journées, ils seroient obligés d'aller servir de manoeuvre ou de travailler à la terre." Ibid.

14. Ibid., *plainte* (14 August 1761). It is not clear why the four firms were victimized. If the quantity of hare and other pelts imported by hatting firms in the following year (1762) are any guide, one of the four (Louis Carbonnel) was the largest manufacturer in the city. The amounts imported by the three others (Jacques Marcou, Pierre Chabrery, and Joseph and Henri Chabaud) were not any larger than those of many other hatting enterprises (A.D. Bouches-du-Rhône, 367E²⁵² [25 June 1762]). The figures may, however, be distorted by the effects of the dispute.

the confraternity of Sainte-Catherine de Sienne were seized, and a sum of 304 livres 18 sous was taken from its deputy treasurer, Joseph Bonafoux.[15] The ensuing trial served, however, to reveal some sympathy for the journeymen's case among the *échevins*. A dozen journeymen appeared as witnesses, as well as six women who worked in the trade as croppers (*tondeuses*). Depositions were taken from only six manufacturers, and little effort appears to have been made to convict individuals of specific violations of the law (which in this instance consisted of the royal letters patent of 2 January 1749 prohibiting combinations).[16] Most of the evidence centered upon the identity and purpose of the journeymen's confraternity. One forty-nine-year-old journeyman stated that he had contributed to the association since 1733. The money was, he said, designed to help the ill, so that the size of the contribution varied according to the number of individuals in need.[17] Evidence of this kind appears to have been accepted, and the *échevins* issued a sentence in March 1762 in which eleven of the twelve journeymen were acquitted and Bonafoux was condemned to the modest fine of 3 livres for having taken the office of deputy treasurer of the confraternity illegally. The verdict maintained the journeymen's right to assemble once a year to elect their officials and to collect 1 sou a week for the relief of the poor and the ill. The confiscated papers and money were returned, with the proviso that the journeymen would make no mention of the word *société* in the record of any of their future deliberations.[18]

Predictably, the masters refused to accept this anodyne judgment and appealed to the Parlement in Aix. The case dragged on for two more years, generating a substantial number of printed *mémoires* and *factums* (all regrettably lost),

15. Ibid.
16. A.C. Marseille, HH 399.
17. "Depuis l'année mil sept cent trente trois il paye l'imposition des garçons chapeliers, laquelle est établie pour secourir les malades et qui varie suivant leur nombre." A.C. Marseille, FF 370.
18. A.C. Marseille, FF 371 (3 March 1762).

before the court produced a verdict that effectively upheld the ruling of the *échevins* of Marseille. The corporation was condemned to the costs of the appeal and found itself forced to raise a loan of 2,000 livres to meet them.[19] Although the Parlement emphasized the illegality of assemblies concerned with wages, it confirmed the recognition given to the confraternity of Sainte-Catherine de Sienne and authorized the journeymen's annual assembly for the purpose of elections to the *oeuvre pie*.[20]

The cycle of stoppages and litigation that ended with this verdict differed from previous disputes in the hatting trade in that it made explicit the links between journeymen in the three cities. Journeymen in Lyon invoked the wages paid in Paris in their dispute, and journeymen in Marseille did the same with the rates paid to hatters in Lyon. Nor were these references a matter of indirect information. Fragments of what was undoubtedly a durable and extensive network of information survive in the archives in Brussels. A letter sent by the Parisian journeymen to the hatters of Brussels in 1762 called for financial support for their counterparts in Lyon. It referred to the litigation undertaken by the journeymen of Lyon before the Parlement of Paris to, as the letter put it, uphold the scale of piece rates justly set by the court and maintain the prices they were paid. Costs of the case had already become substantial, and the Parisian journeymen stated that they had contributed over 600 livres. The purpose of the action, they concluded, was to ensure that journeymen in Lyon were paid the wages that were their due.[21]

---

19. A.D. Bouches-du-Rhône, 367E²⁵⁴, fol. 147 (19 March 1764).
20. A.D. Bouches-du-Rhône, B 5633 (20 February 1764).
21. "Nous sommes obligés de vous donner avis au sujet du procest que les compangnons de Lyon ont avec leur maître. Comme nous voyons que c'est une mauvaise volonté de leur part de ne pas conformer à une arrest sy justement rendue que nos Messieurs du Parlement a jugé à propos, il rejimbe contre et l'ont interjetée. Comme nous voyons que c'est pour soutenir le prix et que nous avonts deja fait pour plus six cens livres de frais et il nous requiere pour leur ayder dans le reste de la procédure, nous avonts jugé apropos de vous le faire sçavoir pour que vous leurs aydiez de ce qu'il

The tone of the letter was echoed in statements made during the second great cycle of conflict, which took place a decade later. Like the conflict of the early 1760s, it drew upon links between journeymen in different localities, so that the sequence of events in the trade passed from one center to another in an almost uninterrupted process.

---

se poura à votre pouvoir. C'est pour soliciter vos frères que des maîtres veulent reteindre en leur payant pas le sçalaire qu'il leur est dû." Archives générales du royaume, Brussels, Corps de métier 465 (12 February 1762).

9

Mercury, Work, and Wages

The *arrêt* issued by the Parlement of Provence in February 1764 lifted the uncertainty surrounding the status of the confraternity of Sainte-Catherine de Sienne. Encouraged by their success, the journeymen of Marseille began to assemble publicly and to have their formal deliberations recorded by a notary. The ensuing record forms an unbroken sequence running from 1765 until the Revolution.[1] The figures of attendance, apparently low in the light of the total number of journeymen working in the trade, are in fact a reflection of the number of *fabriques* that sent delegates to the assemblies (fig. 8). The rise and fall of the number of individuals present closely follows the state of the confraternity's relationship with the masters' corporation. When numbers were low, so too was tension in the trade. When they were high, antagonism between masters and journeymen was more acute. Assemblies of over forty amounted to the representation of some two-thirds of the *fabriques* in Marseille.

The annual assemblies that the journeymen held to elect the priors of the confraternity were not the only occasion on which they met. It is clear that the charitable foundation devoted to the Luminaire de Sainte-Catherine de Sienne concealed a more shadowy, separate organization representing what was termed the *généralité des garçons, compagnons, et ouvriers chapeliers de la ville de Marseille*. It too had its own officials, who were never the same as those of the confraternity. Its deliberations were usually held in private, and only a very small number of them were recorded by a notary.

---

1. There was no assembly in 1788, when the confraternity was again outlawed.

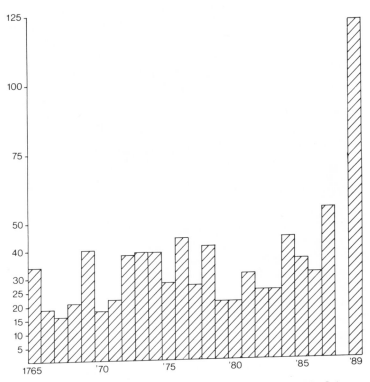

Fig. 8. Numbers present at elections to the Luminaire de Sainte-Catherine de Sienne of the journeymen hatters of Marseille (1765–89). Figures are based on A.D. Bouches-du-Rhône, 358E[201–25].

Although the journeymen insisted, when challenged, that all their assemblies were concerned with the charitable purposes of the confraternity, there are enough traces of meetings of the second association to indicate that this was not true. Only in 1789, when the confraternity had been abolished and the revolutionary crisis had limited the effectiveness of the municipal authorities, did this semiclandestine association meet openly. In March of that year, 122 journeymen assembled to elect their deputies to an assembly of the Third Estate, and 100 took part in a deliberation in April

1789 that decided to offer volunteers for what was to become the National Guard.[2] Throughout the twenty-five-year period between 1765 and 1789, the *généralité des garçons chapeliers* was a constant presence in the life of the trade.

Not only did the ruling of 1764 encourage the journeymen to meet publicly (at least to perform those activities authorized by the Parlement), it also persuaded them to raise the question of the *eau de composition* and its legality. Formally, the provisions of the royal *arrêt* of 1735 still obtained, but in subsequent decades the hatters' corporation of Marseille, like its counterpart in Lyon, had abandoned its hostility to the use of the solution to enable master hatters to obtain a reasonable felt from hare fur.[3] The journeymen were still opposed to its use. In October 1764 the confraternity's three priors presented a memorandum to the *échevins* of Marseille complaining that in the past three years master manufacturers had taken to using certain hitherto unknown and noxious drugs in the preparation of the materials used in the trade. Every worker, they claimed, could attest to the harmful effects of the practice.[4]

Exposure to the solution, they reported, resulted in violent headaches, nausea, and loss of control of the movements of one's limbs. Women's gold rings had been corroded and had had to be replaced or repaired at their employers' expense. Fear of death had caused a general outcry among the men and women working in the trade.[5] One of the doctors at the Hôpital général, which had admitted seven or eight workers affected by the solution, produced evidence to support the

---

2. A.D. Bouches-du-Rhône, 358E²²⁵, fols. 197v and 259 (24 March and 16 April 1789).

3. See above, chapter 6.

4. "Depuis environ trois ans, les maîtres fabriquants employent dans leurs fabriques pour le mélange de leurs matières des drogues à eux inconnues qui nuisent considérablement à la santé. . . . Il n'est plus un ouvrier ni ouvrière qui n'en ait ressenti les funestes effets." A.C. Marseille, FF 373 (15 October 1764).

5. "Un cri général s'est élévé parmi tous les ouvriers et ouvrières. Chacun craint de périr dans le travail que la nécessité les force d'entreprendre." Ibid.

journeymen's claims. Those afflicted, he stated, suffered from a trembling of all parts of the body, which left them unable to use their hands or even remain seated.[6] He opined that the condition had been caused by exposure to mercury dissolved in nitric acid or spirit of niter. Those most affected were the women who removed or carded fur from pelts treated with the solution and the felters who bowed the fur to form *capades* prior to the felting process. His evidence was reinforced by the testimony of one of the doctors of the Oeuvre de la miséricorde, a charitable association for home relief, whose *quartier* contained the majority of workers in the hatting trade. He described the same symptoms of nausea and uncontrollable shaking and declared that the men and women affected were suffering from a convulsive illness caused by particles of mercury and arsenic given off by the solution. The claims of both religion and humanity, he concluded, required the suppression of the invention.[7]

Faced with such charges the corporation agreed to allow an investigation into the alleged effects of the solution. Its previous hostility to the *eau de composition* was now, however, very much a thing of the past. Its own attitude was clear. Properly used, the drugs were entirely harmless and had contributed much to the trade's reputation for fine-quality goods in foreign markets. The corporation decided to begin legal proceedings to legitimize the use of the solution.[8] Matters appear, however, to have rested there for the remainder of the decade. The question of mercury was only

6. "Un tremblement de toutes les parties de leurs corps qui les mettoient hors d'état de se servir de leurs mains et même de se tenir sur le séant." Ibid.

7. "La maladie qui regne parmy les ouvriers chapelliers de l'un et de l'autre sexe est une maladie convulsive causée par les parties mercurielles et arsenicales de la composition dont ils se servent. . . . L'humanité et la religion sont également intéressées à la suppression de cette invention." Ibid.

8. "Lesdits drogues, bien employées, loin de nuire aux ouvriers et maîtres que les préparent et les employent, ont extremmement contribué à mettre dans les lustres la fabrication de chapeaux de Marseille dans l'étranger." A.D. Bouches-du-Rhône, 367E²⁵⁴, fol. 799 (23 October 1764); ibid., fol. 811 (29 October 1764).

revived in the aftermath of a major dispute in the hatting trade of Lyon that encouraged the journeymen in Marseille to renew their own campaign.

The dispute in Lyon began in the autumn of 1769. It centered again on the journeymen's demand to be paid at the same rates as journeymen in Paris. They also claimed that manufacturers in Lyon were willfully violating the terms of the *arrêts* of 1761 and 1762 by paying rates for hats made of wool or other furs when they were in fact beaver hats. The problem was of course that no hat was made exclusively of beaver fur and the use of beaver was becoming more and more limited. What was at issue was therefore the proportion of beaver fur needed to define a hat as a *castor* rather than a *demi-castor*, or a *marcassin* or *vigogne* rather than a *chapeau commun*. Litigation over the matter continued episodically for almost five years, partly because it became enmeshed in the disarray surrounding the status of the Parlements in the last years of the reign of Louis XV.[9] As it became apparent that the question of the composition of a hat was almost impossible to resolve (or even use as the basis of clear argument), both the journeymen and the masters shifted their positions to other, less ambiguous issues. The journeymen increasingly emphasized the need for higher piece and day rates on the felting and finishing sides of the trade respectively. In reply, the masters abandoned their earlier adherence to fixed scales of piece rates and uniform day rates and, instead, argued for free and private negotiation within a universal system of piece rates. These tactical shifts were also an acknowledgment of the growing strategic importance of rural production, with its attendant effects upon the price of finished goods and the supply of labor within the urban economy.[10]

In August 1769 a summons in the name of the two journeymen Chabanon and Deloeuvre, who had been the principal

9. See, for the local effects of Maupeou's policies, Paul Metzger, *Le Conseil supérieur et le Grand Bailliage de Lyon (1771–1774)* (Lyon, 1913).
10. See above, chapter 6.

parties to the litigation of 1761–62, was served upon the corporation, ordering it to pay the rates fixed by the *arrêts* of 1761 and 1762. Both sides began legal proceedings and appealed to the Consulat. In September the court ordered the enforcement of the *tarif* (as it was obliged to because it was a lower court); it also invited each party to nominate three representatives to form a committee that would specify the content of the disputed types of hats. The journeymen duly elected their three delegates; the masters refused. The names of the three men chosen by the *compagnons*—Jean-Pierre Simard, François Chapet, and Ambroise Debarl—are of some importance. The first two were to play a prominent part in the life of the trade for the next twenty years.

The refusal of the corporation to cooperate with the Consulat led to a series of stoppages and finally to a total desertion of all the *fabriques* in the trade for nearly four months.[11] The first to be affected was the firm of Canouville et Delorme, whose twenty-eight journeymen walked out on 25 January 1770. Six of them were arrested and held in prison for twenty-four hours. On 5 February the entire workforce of the trade walked out. Three successive sentences by the Consulat ordering them back to work were ignored. Instead, the journeymen appealed to the Parlement of Paris and sent a deputation to the capital to brief their lawyers.[12] Their case rested upon the rates set by the Parlement in 1761 and 1762. The journeymen insisted that, to end any ambiguity over the content of hats, master hatters should be required to mark each type of hat with a clear symbol. Failure to pay the rates set for each type would entitle a journeyman to hand in his notice and receive a signed certificate of good conduct (*congé*) when he wished. Work would resume, the journeymen stated, when the masters indicated their willingness to abide by these conditions.[13]

Meanwhile in Lyon itself most of the journeymen found

11. A.N. F^{12} 768.
12. A.D. Rhône, 3E 9715 (3 May 1770).
13. A.N. X^{1a} 4672, fol. 338 (29 March 1770); X^{1a} 8202, fol. 1v (23 April 1770).

work digging a road at 18 sous a day, less than half of what they normally earned. The city was placed under an embargo, and itinerant journeymen were discouraged from stopping to find work there. In July it was reported that the annual number of between 120 and 140 journeymen arriving in the city had dwindled to almost none. Only two or three individuals had stopped in the city during the previous six months.[14]

Although the journeymen returned to work at the end of April 1770, the atmosphere in the trade remained tense. In June the corporation complained about the hostility displayed by journeymen toward their masters since the resumption of work and decided to have copies of the letters patent of 2 January 1749 posted all over the city.[15] Migrant workers were still discouraged from stopping in Lyon. In August the corporation reported that, prior to the dispute, the trade had employed some four to five hundred men as felters. At present, there were no more than 240, all working in a decidedly halfhearted way. Demand for labor was such, it stated, that there was employment available for a good five hundred individuals, but the journeymen who, in normal circumstances, would have arrived to take on the work had been prevented from doing so by workers already domiciled in Lyon.[16]

The stoppage entailed a number of separate legal actions. In the first, the Parlement was presented with a further appeal by the journeymen to have the rates for making hats brought into line with those in Paris. The journeymen also

14. A.N. F¹² 768.

15. "Depuis que les ouvriers ont réintégrés les ateliers, ils n'ont cessé de se répandre en mauvais propos contre les maîtres." A.D. Rhône, 3E 5098 (248) (15 June 1770).

16. "Avant les difficultés que se sont élevés entre les ouvriers et nous la fabrique d'icy occupoit de quatre à cinq cens. Actuellement à peine y en a t il 240, sans la moindre émulation. Cette différence est d'autant plus prejudiciable que s'il y en avoit actuellement cinq cens, ils seroient tous occupés. Il n'y a pas de doutte que ce nombre se trouveroit icy sans les menaces les plus audacieuses des ouvriers domiciliés icy, qui ne veullent permettre à aucun ouvrier passager de s'arrêter." A.N. F¹² 768, Chabert, *syndic*, to *contrôleur général des finances* (3 August 1770).

called again upon the court to specify the content of each type of hat and order manufacturers to pay their wages at weekly rather than monthly intervals.[17] Their delegates, notably Simard and Chapet, were also involved in a second appeal (this time in the criminal division of the Parlement) against a warrant for their arrest issued in April 1770 by the Consulat of Lyon. A third suit, undertaken by the hatters' corporation in the Consulat of Lyon against Simard, Chapet, and four other journeymen for violating the letters patent of 1749, also found its way to the Parlement.

Throughout 1771 and into the spring of 1772, journeymen continued to behave in a manner that, as a later court ruling put it, was contrary to the laws of the kingdom, free trade, and the natural subordination owed by inferiors to their superiors.[18] Migrant workers continued to be turned away from the city, while journeymen in Lyon continued to collect money to support their legal actions. It was reported that anyone who refused to contribute was denied access to work either in Lyon or in any other city of the kingdom. Early in May 1772 all the journeymen employed by a manufacturer named Ferreol walked out, resuming work only when he agreed to pay them the rates they demanded. They also demanded—and were granted—fortnightly rather than monthly paydays.[19] The result was a fourth legal action. By then, the Parlement of Paris had been suspended, and the case was transferred to the new Conseil supérieur of Lyon. According to the magistrates of the council, the plethora of litigation was designed to add to the imbroglio by provoking conflict between different courts over their respective competence. The journeymen's tactics were designed to establish a position of impunity by transferring cases between the Parlement and the new court and by then

17. The demands are summarized in the *arrêt* ending the proceedings (A.N. X^{1a} 4739 [4 February 1774]).

18. "Une telle conduite étant contraire à la disposition des lettres patentes du 2 janvier 1749, à la subordination que doit naturellement l'inférieur à son supérieur, aux loix du Royaume si sagement établies et à la liberté du commerce." A.N. X^{1b} 9766 (6 October 1772).

19. A.D. Rhône, 3E 5100 (209) (15 May 1772).

challenging the competence of each when circumstances seemed propitious.[20]

In May 1773 the corporation was forced to recognize its incapacity to prevent a repetition of the events of 1770. If it adopted a firm position in the present circumstances, it noted, it was likely to find its members' workshops deserted and the trade at a halt.[21] Accordingly, it decided to adopt a different strategy. It abandoned all attempts to maintain a uniform scale of piece rates. Henceforth, or at least until the Parlement produced its final verdict, its members were free to come to their own arrangements on the rates they paid. The capitulation was accompanied by a warning that, since workers were not entitled to violate previous rulings by the Parlement or use violence of any kind, the corporation would act vigorously against any such tyranny (*contre une telle tirannie*).[22]

Matters did not, however, end there. In September 1773, doubtless encouraged by the success of the felters, journeymen on the finishing side of the trade began their own campaign. They obtained a ruling from the Consulat increasing their daily rate from 30 to 32 sous 6 deniers. More importantly, they were also accorded an hour for each of their three meals instead of a half hour for the morning and afternoon breaks and an hour at midday as the court had ruled in 1761.[23] The corporation decided to pursue its strategy of opposition to fixed rates and appealed. When it became clear that the Consulat would insist upon some specific rate, the masters modified their position again. They decided to press for the replacement of the daily rate paid to finishers by a piece rate.

20. A.N. X[1b] 9766 (6 October 1772). There were also several other actions between individual employers and their journeymen (see A.N. X[1a] 8216, fol. 232 [4 September 1770]; X[1b] 8418 [19 August 1772]); X[1b] 9766 [22 August 1772]).

21. "Si elle se roidit dans les circonstances actuelles des choses, elle se met dans le cas de voir ses atteliers déserts et de voir retomber dans la plus grande inaction le commerce de la chapellerie de Lyon." A.D. Rhône, 3E 5101 (184) (11 May 1773).

22. Ibid.

23. A.D. Rhône, 3E 5101 (375) (9 September 1773).

Their argument was presented in a long memorandum directed at what the corporation claimed were the disastrous effects of the two *arrêts* of 1761 and 1762 (which, it should be recalled, it had promoted). The corporation stated that it could prove that, prior to the rulings, a manufacturer employing thirty workers on the felting side of the trade needed no more than five or six men to finish the hats that they made. Since then at least ten or a dozen finishers had come to be needed to finish the work of the same thirty felters.[24] They proposed to generalize a system of payment by the piece that was already usual for a small category of workers on the finishing side of the trade. The latter were often masters working on piece rates (*à façon*) on the periphery of the trade, who were taken on periodically to carry out some of the simpler finishing operations when orders were particularly heavy. These workers, who were called *dresseurs*, were paid at rates varying from 12 to 18 sous per dozen hats. The corporation proposed that the piece-rate system be extended to include all but the most routine operations. The daily rate of 32 sous 6 deniers would be paid for coating, brushing, touching up dye, attending to the vats, or delivering goods.[25] All other types of work were to be paid by the piece. It set out a scale of rates for a hypothetical working day:

3 dozen ordinary hats	12 sous per dozen
2½ dozen half-beavers, or *marcassins*	15 sous per dozen
2 dozen beavers or ¼ beavers	18 sous per dozen

The new system would promote emulation and hard work and undermine what the corporation claimed was the

24. "Les maîtres sont en état de prouver que avant ces arrêts un fabriquant qui avoit trente ouvriers à la foule n'occupoit que cinq ou six approprieurs pour approprier les chapeaux que faisoient ces trente fouleurs. Actuellement avec trente ouvriers fouleurs on est obligé d'avoir au moins dix à douze approprieurs." A.C. Lyon, HH 32, "Mémoire des maîtres chapeliers" (September 1773).

25. "On payeroit à la journée de 32s 6d pour faire rober, bagueter, brosser et lustrer la teinture et tenir les bassins, ainsi que pour faire les commissions." Ibid.

subversive influence of incompetent workers. As an illustration of its projected benefits, it referred to the example of the felting side of the trade. Before 1760, it claimed, felters had pressed their claims for higher piece rates by insisting that even the most robust individual was incapable of making more than nine fine-quality hats a week. After the *arrêts* of 1761 and 1762, however, the journeymen had begun making twelve hats. The results, according to the corporation, had been entirely beneficial. The journeymen had raised their output by a quarter. They were earning more. They were all employed. There had been no recriminations.[26] After the events of the past three years, it was a somewhat disingenuous argument. From the journeymen's viewpoint, what had happened was a reduction in piece rates as the beaver content of hats was progressively reduced and a corresponding pressure to increase output in order to maintain earnings.

In February 1774 the Parlement of Paris finally produced its judgment on the original dispute.[27] The verdict upheld the masters' position on every point and condemned the journeymen to the intimidating sum of 3,980 livres in costs. Armed with this victory, the corporation could afford to be magnanimous. It agreed to reduce the amount to which the journeymen had been condemned to 2,000 livres and allow their principal spokesman, Jean-Pierre Simard, to be freed of a prison sentence when the sum was paid.[28] It also set out to consolidate its victory by confirming its decision to abandon a uniform scale of piece rates across the trade. In a formal deliberation, it announced that it was now absolutely impos-

26. "Les ouvriers fouleurs qui en 1760 voulurent faire augmenter le prix des façons des chapeaux soutenoient que l'homme le plus robuste ne pouvait faire plus de neuf chapeaux fins par semaine afin de porter la façon à un prix plus haut, et ils en firent en effet pendant longtemps que neuf au lieu de douze que les maîtres vouloient leur faire faire. . . . Qu'en est-il resulté? Ils font un quart d'ouvrage de plus; ils gagnent tous davantage; ils sont tous occupés et il n'y a jamais eu de reste." A.C. Lyon, HH 32.
27. A.N. X¹ᵃ 4739 (4 February 1774).
28. It is not clear when Simard was imprisoned. A warrant was issued for his arrest in April 1770. He appears to have spent some time in Paris after then, to escape arrest (see chapter 11).

sible to establish a workable *tarif*. It had become a matter of the highest importance to be rid of the entire system because standard scales merely gave rise to daily litigation between masters and journeymen.[29] Faced with the inability of the journeymen to pay anything toward the costs of the case, the masters later imposed a deduction of 10 sous a week on the wages of each *compagnon fouleur* for a period of ten weeks.[30] The workers on the felting side of the trade were effectively eliminated as a collective force in Lyon for a decade. The reverberations of the dispute were, however, very soon apparent in Marseille.

29. "Il seroit de la dernière impossibilité de la mettre à l'exécution. . . . Il engendroit journellement des procès entre les ouvriers et leurs maîtres. . . . Il est de la dernière conséquence de s'en défaire." A.D. Rhône, 3E 5102 (13 May 1774).

30. Ibid. (7 July 1774).

10

The Redefinition of
the Public Sphere

Marseille was the last center of the hatting trade in which working practices were embedded in the prescriptions of the law. Despite the corporation's adoption of the *eau de composition* and its acceptance of the use of mercury in the solution, the statutes of the trade continued to define a working day limited to the production of two hats. During the dispute of 1761, the corporation had even invoked article 38 of the statutes of 1746 to fine a manufacturer who had agreed to increase his journeymen's rates on condition that they produced three hats a day.[1] This action was a useful tactical device during a dispute over the level of piece rates. In the eyes of many masters, however, the new preparations used in the trade made the article an anachronism. Higher levels of productivity now existed in Lyon (or so the hatters there had claimed). They appeared to have been sanctioned by the *arrêt* of the Parlement of Paris of February 1774 and its unqualified support for the hatters of Lyon. The pressure to modify established working practices was therefore considerable. As a result, the journeymen found themselves faced with the problem of defending article 38 of their masters' statutes.

It was probably not a coincidence that they began their campaign soon after the *arrêt* of the Parlement of Paris confirmed the defeat of the journeymen in Lyon. At the beginning of Lent in 1774, there was a meeting in an inn called Les Deux Palmes to prepare for the impending conflict. The

---

1. A.D. Bouches-du-Rhône, 367E²⁵¹, fol. 764 (16 September 1761).

journeymen decided to increase their weekly levy to 6 sous. One of those present later testified that in every *fabrique* the most senior worker, known as the *goret*, was responsible for collecting the sum from each worker.[2] News of the levy spread through the trade. Its purpose was clear, and so was the journeymen's intent to bide their time until manufacturers had accumulated sufficiently large stocks of pelts for the effects of a stoppage to be most damaging. Signs of the tension in the trade are visible in a comment by a manufacturer's wife early in Lent. She was reported to have said that if the masters agreed to shut their shops for three months, the workers would soon come running.[3]

The first victim was a *fabricant* named Giraud, who was reputed to have over 50,000 livres' worth of pelts in stock by early May.[4] It was said that he could not offer much resistance before either capitulating or going bankrupt because his pelts had been destroyed by worms.[5] On the Sunday after all his journeymen had walked out, a crowd gathered outside his *fabrique*, dancing and jostling one another to the mocking beat of a drum.[6] One observer remarked that a long time would pass before Giraud had any workers.[7]

The journeymen requested and were granted the right to meet publicly to discuss conditions in the trade and draw up their grievances. The *échevins* insisted on limiting the size of the gathering to fifteen. The meeting took place on 6 June 1774.[8] The fifteen men, representing the *généralité des garçons*

2. "Dans chaque fabrique il y a le plus ancien ouvrier que l'on nomme vulgairement le gorret [i.e., goret], qui est chargé de faire chaque semaine la collecte de six sols par ouvrier." A.C. Marseille, FF 383, deposition of Joseph Perducet.

3. "Si les maîtres étoient tous d'accord et qu'ils fermassent leurs boutiques pendant trois mois, ils verroient venir les ouvriers." Ibid., deposition of Marie Dejean.

4. A.D. Bouches-du-Rhône, 367E^{262}, fol. 301 (3 May 1774).

5. A.C. Marseille, FF 383, deposition of Jean Blanc.

6. "Avec un tambour et en faisant le branle comme pour l'insulter." Ibid., *plainte des syndics* (20 June 1774).

7. "Avant que ce fabricant eut des ouvriers, il s'en passeroit encore beaucoup de tems." Ibid., deposition of Marie Floux.

8. A.D. Bouches-du-Rhône, 357E^{215}, fol. 196 (6 June 1774).

chapeliers, compagnons, et ouvriers de cette ville, began by referring to the high price of foodstuffs and the exorbitant
level of rents in Marseille. This, it was said, had led them
to send letters to Paris and Lyon to find out the rates paid
to journeymen there. They had learned that in Lyon fine-
quality hats were paid at the rate of 20 to 25 sous each and
ordinary mixed hats at between 15 and 18 sous, while the
rates in Paris ran from 20 to 30 sous for the best-quality
hats to 18 to 20 sous for the rest. In Marseille, however,
fine-quality hats were produced for 14 sous and the rate for
ordinary sorts ran from 10 to 12 sous. A difference of such
magnitude, the assembly noted, had fixed the workers'
attention.

This opening was no more than the appropriate (and rhe-
torically conventional) prelude to the real issue. It was true,
the journeymen continued in tones of delicate irony, that
the master hatters had sought to better their journeymen's
lot by instructing them to make three or four hats a day. But
a worker was incapable of good quality work if he made
more than two hats a day unless he was prepared to exhaust
himself and ruin his health.[9] The force of the argument had
been recognized so clearly, they added, that article 38 of the
statutes expressly prohibited any master from giving out
more materials than were needed to produce two hats in a
day. There was therefore no alternative to higher rates as
the solution to present concerns (*pour remédier aux objets
présents*). The journeymen decided to seek to bring rates in
Marseille into line with those in Lyon and Paris and to continue to abide by article 38 of the corporation's statutes.
They selected three men—Louis-Jacques Martin, Jacques
Rougon, and Joseph Maurel—to be their delegates on all

---

9. "Il est vray que les maîtres voudroient rendre leur état plus heureux
en les obligeant de faire de trois à quatre chapeaux par jour. Mais un
ouvrier ne peut point faire de la bonne besogne quand il fait au dela de
deux chapeaux, à moins qu'il ne veuille épuiser ses forces et ruiner sa
santé." Ibid.

future undertakings on the matter and also agreed to reduce the amount of the weekly levy from 6 to 3 sous.[10]

The deliberation was not received well by the corporation. It assembled on 9 June to be told by its *premier syndic* that it was monstrous to see mere journeymen (*des garçons*) meet, collect money, and, as a body, declare war upon their masters.[11] Claims that the rates in Marseille should be the same as those in Lyon or Paris were groundless, both because of the difference between the types of hat made in the latter two cities and because of the higher cost of living there. Prices in Marseille had, the *syndic* claimed, been higher during the previous year, yet there had been no complaints from the workers. Prices were now substantially lower, and it was obvious from the collections that the workers were far from destitute.[12] The final outrage, he said, was the journeymen's invocation of article 38 of the statutes, which had nothing whatsoever to do with them and was relevant solely to the internal administration of the corporation. The conclusion was predictable. The journeymen's aim was to work as little as possible for as much pay as they could get.[13]

Three weeks later the corporation drew the logical conclusion and abolished article 38 of its statutes. The deliberations were conducted on a suitably elegiac note. The article dated from a time when the use of the fur of hares had been prohibited. Then, no one in Marseille knew how to treat the pelts of rabbits and hares with a solution of mercury and

10. Neither Rougon nor Maurel was an official of the Luminaire de Sainte-Catherine de Sienne. Martin was chosen as one of its priors in February 1775; the other two continued as delegates of the *généralité* (see A.D. Bouches-du-Rhône, 358E[211] and 358E[212], fols. 230 and 1321 [23 February 1775 and 24 November 1776]).

11. "C'est un monstre que de voir des garçons s'assembler, se cottiser et déclarer en corps la guerre contre leurs maîtres." A.D. Bouches-du-Rhône, 367E[264], fol. 358 (9 June 1774).

12. "Les ouvriers ne se plaignoient pas. Aujourd'hui le taux en est diminué de beaucoup. Les garçons et ouvriers sont si peu dans la misère qu'ils se cottisent pour plaider." Ibid.

13. "Leur objet est de peu travailler et d'être bien payés." Ibid.

nitric acid. Since that time, however, the technique of using mercury dissolved in nitric acid to treat the pelts of hares and rabbits, devised by the English, adopted in France, and justified by the abbé Nollet, had succeeded finally in overcoming the obstacles of prejudice and outdated custom.[14] The hatters of Marseille had come to equal and even surpass the English in the quality and beauty of the hats they produced. There was no alternative. The way was open. All that was needed was to follow the path. Many had already begun.[15] After this rhetorical crescendo—in which the familiar tropes of the Enlightenment were combined with an appeal to the realities of the world market—the hatters decided to raise the minimum number of hats produced in a day from two to three.

By then, the *échevins* had begun to take depositions on the dispute. The hearings, which continued until 12 July, contain a rich series of images of individual and collective behavior. They reveal the geographical distribution of the *fabriques* deserted by their journeymen: rue des Grands-Carmes, rue de la Pierre-qui-Rage, and, predictably, rue des Chapeliers. They disclose too those points of social intercourse where masters and journeymen encountered one another outside the workplace: the *cabarets* of course, such as the one entered by the hapless master Giraud. He found a group of journeymen already seated; they invited him to drink with them and offered him food. While he was seated with them, one of the men began to reproach him, accusing him of having had his brothers imprisoned. He was told that he had worked like an idiot (*jean foutre*) and that he was one himself.[16] He was, the journeymen observed, no longer on

---

14. "La manière de secréter les peaux de lièvre et de lapin par le secours du mercure dissous dans l'eau forte imaginé par les Anglois, adopté en France et justifié par M. l'abbé Nollet dans son *Art du Chapelier*, est enfin parvenue à vaincre dans Marseille les obstacles que le préjugé et la vieille coutume y aportoient." Ibid., fol. 428 (30 June 1774).

15. "La voye est ouverte. Nous n'avons besoin que de la suivre. Elle l'est déjà." Ibid.

16. "Il avoit travaillé comme un j—— f—— et qu'il l'étoit." A.C. Marseille, FF 383, deposition of Louis Ferraud.

his own premises, but in a place frequented by everyone, *et qu'ils luy f——— sur le nez*. Barbers' shops were another public place. The same Giraud found that a visit to his wigmaker to have his wig dressed entailed a long but courteous discussion with a journeyman who was being shaved. The discussion turned upon the chemical used to make hats and the wages given to the workers.[17] Talk in other public places had a different tenor. A sixty-year-old woman who dealt in old clothes overheard a conversation among another group of women while sitting out on a bench. They said that any journeyman hatter unwilling to leave Marseille was likely to be assaulted with staves.[18]

Talk among journeymen was equally varied. Repeated reference was made to the trade in Lyon and Paris. A forty-year-old felter stated that he and his comrades in the trade had agreed that, since the *eau de composition* was extremely bad for their health, they could not be expected to make more than two hats a day. This rate, he added, accorded with the prescriptions of the statutes of Lyon and Paris.[19] Another journeyman reported that shortly after he began working for a *fabricant* named Girouin on the rue des Grands-Carmes, a passing worker came and told all the journeymen that, since the Parisian rule (*le règlement de Paris*) stipulated that no one should make more than two hats a day, they could not make any more.[20]

Frequent reference was also made to the noxious effects

17. "Il étoit question de la drogue qu'on emploie dans la fabrication des chapeaux ou des salaires que l'on donnoit aux ouvriers." Ibid., deposition of Jean-Claude Sataint.

18. "Quand les garçons chapeliers ne vouloient pas partir de la ville, les autres leur donnoient d'un baton." Ibid., deposition of Margueritte Giraud.

19. "Lorsqu'il s'est trouvé avec de ses camarades ouvriers chapeliers . . . ils se disoient entr'eux que l'eau de composition dont se servent les chapeliers . . . étant extrêmement nuisible à la santé, ils ne pouvoient faire davantage que de deux chapeaux par jour, relativement à ce qui est préscrit pour les statuts de Paris et Lyon." Ibid., deposition of Pierre Perrot.

20. "Il passa à la fabrique . . . un ouvrier qui dit à tous les compagnons . . . que le règlement de Paris portant de ne faire que deux chapeaux par jour, ils ne devoient pas faire davantage." Ibid., deposition of Jacques Blanc.

of the *eau de composition*. There were even workers who were unable to use their hands and who had to be fed, stated one journeyman whose own limbs were afflicted by a trembling (*ayant tous les membres tremblotant*). For them, there were no reservations about the right to higher rates. One of six journeymen arrested in October 1774 went so far as to say, when interrogated, that although he had not actually demanded more money, he would certainly be pleased to have a little more. His words were repeated, in the same sardonic vein, by another of the men.[21]

Occasionally the decision to stop work was not an easy one. Journeymen who gave notice found it difficult to offer reasons and only did so, as one witness put it, after hesitating a little or, as another stated, after dreaming for a while. Yet, as one of the journeymen put it, it was necessary to do as the others had done, although the decision could still cause surprise. "Vous aussi, vous voulez sortir," a master exclaimed when his last journeyman handed in his notice. "Oui, nous sommes tous d'un dire, et je veux faire comme les autres," came the reply.[22]

Not all journeymen stopped work. "Tiens, voilà ce quoyon [testicle]," a working journeyman heard shouted at him.[23] Another man, working alongside three apprentices, was told that they were four villains who each deserved six blows from a stave and that they should behave like men.[24] Single men were encouraged to leave Marseille and were given 9 livres to help them on their way.[25] In some cases, their departure brought about real hardship for their dependents. A sixty-year-old widow stated that her only son had left the city after having worked for the same manufacturer

21. "On luy feroit plaisir de lui donner quelque chose de plus." Ibid., interrogation of Jean-Joseph Berard and Joseph Coste.
22. The other French phrases are "après avoir un peu tatonné"; "après avoir rêvé quelque tems"; "qu'il faisoit comme les autres." Ibid.
23. Ibid., deposition of Pierre Fayet.
24. "Qu'ils étoient quatre coquins, qu'ils mériteroient chacun six coups de baton et qu'ils devoient faire comme des hommes." Ibid., deposition of Joseph Maurin.
25. Ibid., deposition of Jacques Blanc.

for over six years and that he had been her only help and breadwinner.[26]

Although the municipal authorities allowed the journeymen's representatives to meet publicly to discuss their demands and some journeymen were convinced that they had the *échevins'* favor, the determination of the corporation to bring its statutes into line with current conditions in the trade tended to prevail. The decision to abandon article 38 of the statutes was accompanied by a modification of the rules concerning apprenticeship. Masters were now able to take on one apprentice a year instead of one at a time for the length of the apprenticeship.[27] This proposal was complemented by a decision to establish a corporate labor exchange (*bureau de placement*) to prevent journeymen from moving from shop to shop without the authority of the corporate employment officer (*embaucheur*).[28] The municipal authority's approval of these decisions forced the journeymen to appeal to the Parlement. They continued too to press their case for a higher wage. In November the corporation was still sufficiently concerned by what it termed the workers' obstinate determination to obtain an increase and by the threat of further generalized walkouts that it nominated four extra officials to assist the *syndics* in the preparation of the case.[29]

Legal maneuver continued throughout the following year. In February 1775 the journeymen were forced to pay the corporation 145 livres out of their common fund to meet the costs of proceedings at the Echevinage.[30] Undeterred, they served a summons on the corporation in July ordering it to enforce article 7 of the statutes against masters who, they claimed, had taken on more apprentices than the one every two years permitted by the article.[31] After taking legal ad-

26. "C'étoit le seul secours que la déposante avoit pour subsister." Ibid., deposition of Margueritte Giraud.
27. A.D. Bouches-du-Rhône, 367E²⁶⁴, fol. 368 (25 May 1774).
28. Ibid., fol. 471 (19 July 1774).
29. "L'obstination des ouvriers à vouloir être augmentés." Ibid., fol. 752 (11 November 1774) and fol. 793v (15 November 1774).
30. Ibid., 367E²⁶⁵, fol. 79v (4 February 1775).
31. Ibid., fol. 543 (19 July 1775).

vice, the corporation decided to ignore the summons on the grounds that the "so-called *généralité des garçons chapeliers*" had no standing. It decided to embark upon action of its own and announced its wish to put an end once and for all to what it called the interminable interference by workers who had absolutely nothing to do with the statutes of the corporation.[32] By December 1775, however, the tone was less belligerent. The case also involved an examination of the use of the *eau de composition*. The delicacy of the subject was reflected in the masters' concern to emphasize that the solution was heavily diluted and that no individual was allowed to use more than an ounce of mercury for every pound of nitric acid, together with at least the same quantity of water. They decided that this specification should be ratified by the Parlement.[33]

The Parlement preferred to bide its time on the question. In May 1776 it referred the question of both the *eau de composition* and the rates paid to journeymen to the arbitration of the municipal authorities.[34] The protracted nature of the case worked to the journeymen's advantage. By June 1776 it had become clear that the decision to establish a corporate labor exchange was a total failure. Faced with complaints by several manufacturers that they had been unable to find any journeymen, the officials of the corporation admitted despairingly that they had such a large number of lawsuits to follow and that they were in such disarray themselves that they could not rescue an institution that had fallen into an even more pronounced state of disarray.[35]

In August 1776 the matter of the *eau de composition* was raised for public arbitration. For three weeks the mayor of

32. "Pour faire cesser une fois pour toutes les tracasseries multipliées et sans fin de ces ouvriers, qui n'ont absolument rien à voir dans le maintien des statuts du corps." Ibid., fol. 596v (1 August 1775).

33. Ibid., fols. 1104v (5 December 1775) and 1189 (29 December 1775).

34. Ibid., 367E[266], fol. 523v (7 May 1776).

35. "Ayant nombre de procès à soutenir, ils ont été assez dérangés pour ne pas faire sortir de son dérangement par eux mêmes une délibération qui étoit tombée en désuétude et qui souffre mille embarras." Ibid., 367E[267], fol. 706 (21 June 1776).

Marseille, accompanied by the *procureur du roi*, solemnly observed a trial demonstration of the process of making hats
with the solution, in order to adjudicate between the respective claims of the masters and journeymen.[36] Each side was
represented by four people: the masters by the four *syndics*
of the corporation; the journeymen by four deputies of the
généralité. The account of the trial demonstration contains a
description of the art of making hats that provides much
indirect information about why journeymen were so reluctant to exceed the statutory limit of two hats a day. It confirms that the pattern of work that Nollet described in the
Parisian hatting trade, involving a pair of felters each working on alternate stages of the felting process, also existed in
Marseille.[37] The details are therefore of some importance.

The trial began with a disaster that indicates how unpre-
dictable and imperfectly understood the whole process of
secrétage was. Three pounds of nitric acid were mixed with
three ounces of mercury and diluted with three pounds of
water. Seven-and-a-half dozen hare pelts were treated with
the solution and, on inspection the following morning,
turned out to be have been scorched by the acid. A chemist
was called and a new solution was prepared, this time diluted with seven-and-a-half pounds of water. Nine dozen
pelts were now treated. The outcome on this occasion was
successful. The pelts were given out to eight women for the
removal of the fur. The fur was then passed to another four
women and carded into two piles of four pounds each. Each
pile was now ready to be made into hats. A dyer was called
and instructed to describe the types of hat that he treated
most frequently. On the basis of his information, the mayor
ordered each side to select two representatives, each of
whom would make three half-beaver hats of five, seven, and
nine ounces respectively. The journeymen demurred, saying
that they would prefer the demonstration to include every
type of hat made in Marseille, so that there would be no

36. A.C. Marseille, FF 386 (13 August 1776 to 2 September 1776).
37. See above, chapter 6.

possibility of uncertainty in defining how much time was needed to make them. Their objection was overruled, and the parties assembled at the beginning of a trial working day to perform the demonstration.

The trial was due to begin at six o'clock in the morning. The parties gathered at five and waited for some time until all the journeymen had arrived. There was a brief (and probably characteristic) delay before the four contestants could get down to work. Eventually the prescribed quantities of fur were weighed out, and the bowing operation began at 6:45. After exactly two hours, the two masters had each prepared the fur for two hats, while both of the journeymen had completed one hat and were each still on the second.

At the break, the journeymen lodged a formal complaint about the way in which the demonstration had been organized. They stated that the working practices that had been followed were not those that were usual in normal circumstances. The details again call for close observation. The journeymen stated that according to the usage observed in every enterprise, there should be one bowing instrument (*arçon*) for two workers.[38] In this instance, however, each participant had been given an *arçon* to use. They announced that they would agree to continue but would not approve what they termed was this new method (*cette nouvelle méthode*).[39] The masters agreed that the normal practice was as the journeymen had described, but they denied that the difference had any bearing upon the time needed to perform the operation. At the most, they said, an additional hour a week would be needed if the work was done according to the established usage. Because the normal working pattern consisted of a series of alternating roles, one journeyman used the bowing instrument while the other "built" his hat. The masters asserted that this pattern entailed a loss of no

---

38. "Suivant l'usage pratiqué dans toutes les fabriques, il n'y a qu'un arçon pour deux ouvriers, et que néanmoins les fabriquans ont affecté de donner un arçon à chacun des maîtres et des ouvriers travaillant." A.C. Marseille, FF 386.

39. Ibid.

more than an hour at the beginning of each week, because one journeyman was always able to work on fur that he had bowed the previous day while his partner used the *arçon* to begin his working day.[40] On Saturdays and the eve of holidays, they concluded, there was always a certain amount of fur waiting to be put into shape.

The objection was duly recorded, and the four returned to the work of making their hats. By midday the two masters and one of the journeymen had completed the initial preparation of three hats, while the second journeyman was still on his second. In the afternoon the *capades* were felted. By 5:25 both the masters had completed their work. The two journeymen finished theirs an hour later. The record noted that they had broken off from their work for ten minutes to have their afternoon drink.[41] Three hats had, nonetheless, been made in a day. They were left to dry overnight, and the work was inspected the following morning. Fearing the worst, the journeymen warned that the final decision over how well or badly the hats had been made could not be taken in Provence.[42] The mayor was indeed obliged to admit that none of the hats looked as fine as a *demi-castor* ordinarily did. This, the masters rather belatedly explained, was because it was customary to use fur from the belly and underthroat of a hare in *demi-castors*.

The account of this somewhat inconclusive trial was referred to the Parlement. The court delayed its final verdict until July 1777, when it ruled in favor of the masters. It authorized the use of the *eau de composition*, although .it

40. "Parce que dans les fabriques un garçon arçone dans le tems que l'autre bâtit, ce qui occasionne tout au plus une perte d'une heure de tems au commencement de la semaine pour la moitié des ouvriers seulement, attendu que ceux qui n'arçonent pas en commençant la journée bâtissent dans le tems que les autres arçonent et opèrent sur le poil qu'ils avoient arçoné la veille." Ibid.

41. "Il est à observer néanmoins que lesdits compagnons ont interrompu leur travail pendant dix minutes qu'ils ont employé à leur gouté." Ibid.

42. "Ce n'étoit pas en Provence qu'il devoit être décidé si les chapeaux dont il s'agit étoient bien ou mal fabriqués." Ibid.

stipulated that the solution should conform to the substances prescribed in Nollet's *Art du chapelier*. The revocation
of article 38 of the statutes was a logical corollary to this
decision. Gratified by its success, the corporation offered to
drop all further litigation, if the journeymen would do the
same.[43]

The journeymen refused to comply. In August 1777
Jacques Rougon called an assembly that was attended by
forty-seven delegates.[44] He recommended that the journeymen accept the *arrêt* of the Parlement. At the same time,
however, they should take further legal action against the
corporation over the question of the number of apprentices
to which each master was entitled. The masters were also to
be compelled to withdraw the warrants that had been issued
against fifteen journeymen during the stoppages of 1774.
The meeting accepted the suggested course of action and
then paid its respects to Rougon. For nearly three years, it
noted, Rougon had worked to promote the rights and interests of the *généralité*.[45] He was invited to continue as the
journeymen's deputy and was promised a weekly income of
9 livres until all the issues that had given rise to the assembly had been settled. The decision to pay Rougon 9 livres a
week was particularly important, the assembly recorded, because the masters had refused to give him any work.

The venomous state of relations in the trade continued
into the following year, when the journeymen appear to
have obtained a sentence fixing piece rates from the *échevins*.
In August 1778 they served a summons on the corporation
ordering it to prevent its members from violating the sentence and, more specifically, from dismissing journeymen at
the beginning of the week instead of the usual Saturday
evenings if they were not prepared to accept the rates pro-

43. A.D. Bouches-du-Rhône, 367E[268], fol. 679 (8 July 1777).
44. Ibid., 358E[213], fol. 813 (3 August 1777).
45. "Depuis près de trois ans ledit Rougon a travaillé et travaille pour le
soutien des droits et de l'intérêt de la généralité. . . . Les maîtres lui refuse
[*sic*] du travail." Ibid.

posed to them.[46] The corporation decided to ignore the demand on the grounds that, as the hatters in Lyon had recently emphasized, it was a matter for the individuals concerned. The selective victimization of journeymen continued. In this, the corporation was also following the example of master hatters elsewhere. Not only did the practice result in the imprisonment of a number of journeymen, it also revealed a great deal about their associations.

46. Ibid., 367E[269], fol. 887v (13 August 1778).

11

Droguins and *Devoirants*

The lockouts and victimization that accompanied the dispute in Marseille were already established practices in Paris and Lyon. In October 1748 the Parisian journeymen informed their counterparts in Brussels that the masters in the capital had organized a lockout to prevent any opposition to the *arrêt* that the corporation had obtained on 31 July. They reported that two hundred journeymen had been laid off in an attempt to starve them into submission.[1]

In Lyon the victimization of two workers led to an incident that reveals much about the specific features of journeymen's associations in the hatting trade. During the dispute of 1770, the corporation had organized a concerted campaign against the journeymen's two principal spokesmen, François Chapet and Jean-Pierre Simard. Simard appears to have escaped arrest by going to work in Paris; he returned to Lyon only in 1774. Four years later he and Chapet were arrested in what was a clear attempt by the corporation to eliminate their influence in the trade.

The event that occasioned their arrest was a violent brawl that took place on Sunday, 26 July 1778, in an inn called the Mouton Couronné in the suburb of Vaise. Between 150 and 200 journeymen hatters invaded the inn and assaulted a group of some 18 other journeymen from a number of different trades: curriers, tanners, joiners, and hatters among them. The next day thirteen of the assailants

---

1. "Ils n'ont sçue mieux faire que de mettre bas depuis le 19 du présent [i.e., October] jusqu'à aujourdhuy les uns après les autres, de sorte que nous sommes deux cens sans ouvrage, croyant par là nous prendre par famine." Archives générales du royaume, Brussels, Corps de métier 465 (31 October 1748).

were arrested, followed three days later by the arrest of Simard and Chapet.

The episode is best understood in the context of the gradual modification of corporate regulation that had occurred since the time of the Seven Years' War. Successive decisions by the courts tended to remove, either explicitly or implicitly, such matters as the content of hats, the rates at which they were paid, the composition of the workforce, and the always nebulous formal status of journeymen, from the public sphere. The master hatters' successful legal action against the journeymen, culminating in the *arrêt* of February 1774, and their subsequent decision to leave the question of working conditions to negotiation between private individuals were indicative of this trend. The plan to extend the system of piece rates paid to the casual workers known as *dresseurs* to everyone working on the finishing side of the trade was a move in the same direction.

The possibility that journeymen working as finishers would be employed on the same basis as men they regarded as casual laborers was sufficiently alarming to lead them to organize their own defense. On 24 November 1776 a clandestine meeting of delegates from twenty-six hatting enterprises took place in an inn called the Moulin au Vent. The meeting was called by Chapet.[2] There the journeymen ratified a series of rules designed to prevent any possible amalgamation of established *approprieurs* with *dresseurs* who were paid by the piece. Anyone employed on the finishing side of the trade would be heavily fined either for working for a master who took on subcontracted work as a *dresseur* or for working alongside a *dresseur* himself. Failure to denounce anyone who did so was also to be heavily fined. There were fourteen rules in all, each designed to maintain a strict quarantine upon casual, unapprenticed workers.

2. "MM vous êtes priés de la part des confrères de vous trouver dimanche 24 novembre entre midi et une heure chez Chapet, au Moulin au Vent, pour y déliberer sur des affaires qui vous intéressent." A.C. Lyon, HH 32. De Francesco wrongly lists the number at nineteen, a figure which, when set against a later assembly of journeymen from thirty-two *fabriques*, leads to a linear, developmental framework of analysis (De Francesco, "Conflittualità sul lavoro," 181).

Significantly, however, the journeymen were careful to make an exception to the quarantine in the case of their own children. It is clear, in other words, that the measures were designed to protect a certain form of family economy that existed among settled and established journeymen. The fear that work might be available to immigrants from rural areas or to itinerant journeymen rather than kin is a significant one and is highly suggestive of the distinctive age-composition and concerns of journeymen in the hatting trade. It points to the importance of continuity of employment in the core of large hatting enterprises as the basis of a career as a small subcontractor on the trade's periphery.

The corporation denounced the irregular assembly to the Consulat, which duly issued a condemnation of the journeymen's rules in June 1777.[3] Matters appear to have remained at this point for a year, until the fight in the Mouton Couronné provided the corporation with an opportunity to eliminate the individuals it deemed responsible for the enduring tension in the trade.

The arrest of Simard and Chapet on 31 July 1778 followed evidence given by a journeyman hatter who was one of the victims of the attack. In his deposition he stated that Simard and Chapet had been the principal instigators of the illegal assemblies of journeymen hatters. The two men, he said, were so dangerous that, even though they were not present, their instructions had been followed by the 150 men who had been involved in the brawl.[4] He added that the two were custodians of a fund of some 750 livres collected from journeymen in the trade, which was designed to meet the costs of lawsuits arising from the assaults that they instigated.[5]

3. A.C. Lyon, HH 32 (18 June 1777).

4. "Les principaux motteurs de toutes ces assemblées illicites sont les nommés Simard et Chapet. . . . Ces deux particuliers sont si dangereux qu'il sait que, sans paraître, c'est eux qui donnent tous les conseils du désordre auquel cette bande de cent cinquante s'est livrée." A.D. Rhône, BP 3449 (27 July 1778), deposition of Jacques Palliet.

5. "La déstination de ces deniers est pour terminer les mauvaises affaires qu'ils pourroient avoir rélativement aux coups qu'ils donneroient." Ibid.

The two individuals singled out as ringleaders were mature men. Chapet was forty-two; Simard, thirty-eight. Chapet presented a statement signed by sixteen of the residents of the building on the rue Poise that he had lived in for the past four years, testifying to the fact that he was known for the quiet life he led and denying that he had ever held any meetings at his home.[6] Simard did the same and also produced a character reference from the firm of Chol et Janin in Paris, one of the largest and most prestigious enterprises in the capital, where he had worked between July 1772 and January 1774. Both men denied any involvement in the incident for which they had been arrested. Simard admitted, however, that he had known Chapet since 1759. He also said that he himself was a member of what, he said, was a sort of association for the welfare of sick journeymen, and he presented a certificate signed by the sacristan of the Franciscan convent of Saint-Loe testifying that journeymen in the hatting trade celebrated mass in the church several times a month. They also celebrated a requiem for deceased members and held a service every year on All Saints Day.[7] He vehemently denied however, that either he or Chapet was the head of the clandestine association of journeymen known as the *droguins*.

His denial of any knowledge of an association of that name was met with incredulity by the authorities. Nor was the name unfamiliar to employers. Several of them used it in presenting requests to the authorities on behalf of journeymen arrested after the brawl. One of them described the fight as a quarrel between *devoirants* and *droguins*.[8] The allusions

6. "[Il] a toujours été en notre connoissance un homme paisible. . . . Il ne s'est tenue aucune assemblée dans son domicile." Ibid.

7. Simard belonged to "une espèce d'association pour soulager les compagnons malades." The sacristan stated that "les compagnons chapeliers font dire dans notre église plusieurs messes par mois et que, lorsqu'ils ont quelqu'un de mort dans leur société, ils font faire un service pour le défunt. Que le jour de la commemoration des morts, le deux de novembre, ils font faire un service." Ibid.

8. Ibid., certificate by Marion *père, fils,* et Gaulmier on behalf of Pierre Saigne (28 July 1778).

are clearly to the *compagnonnages*. Journeymen's associations in the hatting trade were, it would seem, linked in some way to these still mysterious bodies. The nature of these links requires clarification, for until now a certain, perhaps rather misleading, impression of the parallels between the concerns and preoccupations of eighteenth-century journeymen and those of workers in more recent times has been allowed to persist. This impression has its merits, because eighteenth-century journeymen also worked and expected to be able to live from the work that they did. Nonetheless, the situation of eighteenth-century journeymen found its expression in certain characteristic forms of association and ceremonial, which historians have often identified with the equally distinctive rituals and ceremonial of the *compagnonnages*.[9] The circumstances that led to the attack on the Mouton Couronné in 1778 suggest ways of understanding these associations more concretely than has hitherto been possible. As a result, it may be possible to place both the *compagnonnages* and the associations formed by journeymen in the hatting trade in a somewhat different light and begin to identify some of the differences between *compagnons du devoir, gavots, bons enfants,* and *droguins*.

The inn known as the Mouton Couronné in the suburb of Vaise was well known as the meeting place, or *cayenne*, of the *compagnons du devoir*. In 1776 it had been at the center of criminal proceedings when a nearby landowner complained that his servants had been assaulted by some journeymen carpenters when they went there to retrieve his dog.[10] The seigneurial court that dealt with the affair ordered the journeymen to end the activities of the association (which had included a number of mock trials and noisy festivities) and prohibited the inn's owner from taking the title of *mère des compagnons du devoir*. Nevertheless, the attack on the

9. See Truant, "Solidarity and Symbolism Among Journeymen Artisans," and Lecuir, "Associations ouvrières de l'époque moderne," cited above, p. 76n. 20.

10. A.D. Rhône, 134B, *plainte,* Sandrin de Champdieu.

inn two years later was clearly directed at the *compagnons du devoir* lodging there.

Soon after the attack, the Conseil du roi received a petition from twenty-three journeymen hatters on behalf of an unspecified number of others, calling upon the Crown to protect them from similar attacks and to require all master hatters to inform the authorities of any associations among journeymen.[11] In 1777, according to the petitioners, for reasons of jealousy or because of a combination, a number of journeymen domiciled in Lyon had decided to expel from the city migrants from elsewhere.[12] The raid on the inn had been the culmination of this project. All twenty-three of the signatories of the petition were from localities outside Lyon: some from places like Chalon-sur-Saône or Sens, which were relatively near; others from the Limousin, Gascony, or the Agenais, which were very distant.

The *compagnons du devoir* were therefore itinerant journeymen; their assailants were journeymen who were domiciled in Lyon. The *droguins* or *bons enfants* were members of an association made up of men like Chapet and Simard: no longer young and mobile, but often married and in as stable an employment as they could find. There is nothing particularly surprising about this observation. Nor does it mean that the *droguins* were not migrants themselves. It is likely, however, that *their* migrations had taken place earlier in their lives, when they came to Lyon either to serve an apprenticeship or as a prelude to marriage and residence in the city. In the light of conditions in the hatting trade, it is possible to situate these various types of migrant journeymen in a fuller context and, as a result, offer some reasons for the conflict between rival associations. For the tensions that existed in Lyon can also be found in Marseille.

In 1779 one of the journeymen accused of participation in the attack on the Mouton Couronné petitioned the authori-

11. A.N. F^{12} 768, "Requête au roi" (1778).
12. "Plusieurs compagnons de Lyon, soit par jalousie, ou par esprit de cabale, formèrent . . . le projet d'exclure de cette ville les compagnons étrangers qui s'y trouvaient alors." Ibid.

ties against his conviction in absentia in September 1778. He claimed that he had been falsely accused by the victims of the attack. They were, he said, *compagnons du devoir* who had been offended by his refusal to join their association. To avenge themselves, they had brought a malicious prosecution against him, as they had once tried to do in Marseille.[13]

Whatever the details of the feud might have been, the petition indicates that antagonisms among journeymen's associations in the hatting trade also existed in Marseille. Even clearer evidence can be found in an incomplete record of legal proceedings in 1783–84. Early in December 1783 the police authorities in Marseille surprised a meeting of some twenty journeymen in the canteen of the citadel of Saint-Nicolas. They confiscated a small sum of money (23 livres 8 sous) and a bundle of papers. Among the papers was a notebook containing an alphabetical list of the names of the members of an association known as the *gavots*.[14] Shortly afterward, in January 1784, the *généralité des garçons chapeliers* presented a memorandum to a barrister at the Parlement in Aix seeking legal advice on how to obtain authorization for an assembly to raise money to meet the costs of a court case in which they were involved. As the barrister's advice indicates, the proposed levy was to be used to proceed upon a complaint made against the *compagnons du devoir* and, at the same time, to defend the journeymen against an action brought by the *compagnons du devoir* against workers in the hatting trade.[15] He advised them that no mention of this project should be made in their formal request to assemble.

13. "Ceux-ci, compagnons du devoir, irrités de ses refus de former corps avec eux ont executé par devant vous . . . un projet de vengeance qu'ils avoit [*sic*] inutilement tenté à Marseille." A.D. Rhône, BP 3449, petition by Jean François Verly.

14. The incident is mentioned in A.D. Bouches-du-Rhône, 367E²⁷⁷, fol. 238 (18 February 1784).

15. "Pour poursuivre la plainte portée contre les garçons du devoir, et pour deffendre à celle que les garçons du devoir ont porté contre les ouvriers chapeliers." A.C. Marseille, HH 399, "Déliberation de Simeon, avocat au Parlement."

Thus in both Lyon and Marseille there are indications of conflict between *compagnons du devoir* on the one hand, and journeymen known as *droguins, bons enfants,* or *gavots* on the other. From the continuities in the personnel involved, it is clear too that the journeymen who had been involved in disputes with masters in the two cities were attached to the latter association. It was they who made up the *généralité des garçons, compagnons, et ouvriers* in Marseille and were represented by Simard and Chapet in Lyon. Both of the latter were married and, as has been mentioned, neither was particularly young. Accounts by others accused of the attack on the Mouton Couronné of how they spent the evening of the affray reinforces the sense that the *droguins* were older, settled, often married men. One had helped his neighbors to move; another had been out walking with his wife; a third, a thirty-nine-year-old man, had worked until 4 A.M. before returning home to care for one of his four children who was ill with smallpox.[16]

The evidence from Marseille confirms this impression. In the course of disputes in 1761, 1774, and 1785–86, a total of fifty-five journeymen were arrested or gave evidence in court hearings. Twenty-seven of them were over thirty years old, and a relatively large number were men in their middle age or older. Admittedly, the total is small, and it was perhaps easier to identify, arrest, or summon men of fixed abode and family ties than younger, more mobile men. There is nonetheless a clear difference between the ages of the men in this small sample and the ages of the journeymen hatters who registered to find work in the smaller town of Tours between 1782 and 1790.[17] There, thirty-seven of the forty-three people who registered with the police authorities were under the age of thirty. The proportion of mature men in these two, admittedly small, samples amounted to some 13 percent in Tours and almost 50 percent in Marseille. It is likely that a proportion of the men who worked in the hat-

16. A.D. Rhône, BP 3499.
17. A.D. Indre-et-Loire, 5E 788.

ting trade in the three big cities remained journeymen in formal terms for most, if not all, of their working lives.[18] Because of the substantial fixed costs associated with the manufacturing side of the trade, their chief hope of being able to set themselves up to work on their own outside the corporate world lay in the retail or repairing side of the trade. It would seem therefore that one element in the tension between *devoirants* and *droguins* or *gavots* was a division between young and old, between men who were settled and men who were not, and, more fundamentally, between men who were established in the trade in a particular city and men who were not.

Expressed like this, however, the divisions are too neat and too rigid. In reality there was no sharp boundary separating the relatively old from the relatively young, the relatively settled from the relatively transient, and the relatively established from the relatively marginal. The corporation in Lyon estimated in 1770 that there were usually some 150 itinerant journeymen working on the felting side of the trade alone.[19] In normal circumstances, therefore, journeymen who were domiciled in the city and journeymen who were not tended to work together; although distinctions existed, they could obviously be negotiated. It is probable, however, that developments in the hatting trade, especially after the end of the Seven Years' War, undermined the relative stability of these distinctions. Changes in corporate statutes affecting apprenticeship, as had occurred in both Lyon and Marseille, or modifications in the composition of the workforce, such as the use of unapprenticed *dresseurs* and *affermés* proposed in Lyon, were indicative of a broader process that tended to divest the high-quality, beaver-intensive hatting trades of Paris, Lyon, and Marseille of their distinctive characteristics.

As rabbit and hare fur came to displace the fur of beaver, the hatting trades of the three cities came to have more and

18. See above, chapter 5.
19. See above, chapter 9.

more in common with those found in scores of small towns all over France. One result of the removal of the technical obstacle formed by familiarity with beaver fur in the production of fine-quality hats was that journeymen working at the core of the small number of large hatting concerns in the three great cities were faced with a larger number of potential competitors both for immediate employment and, eventually, for a place among the small, subcontracting enterprises on the periphery of the trade. The rules adopted by the journeymen working as finishers in Lyon in 1776 reveal a clear distinction between their desire to keep subcontracted work for themselves and their families, and their determination to destroy that work if it involved outsiders.[20] It was the need to assert distinctions of this kind that lay at the heart of the division between *devoirants* and *droguins*.

This tension between different groups of journeymen in the hatting trade suggests that many of the features of the *compagnonnages* are best understood in terms of relationships among journeymen themselves rather than between journeymen and their masters. Again it is necessary to emphasize that the distinction was relative rather than absolute and that many of the characteristic rituals and procedures of the *compagnonnages* could be, and were, turned against masters. It is probable, however, that their primary audience was an audience of journeymen. A series of incidents spread over a period of more than a hundred years indicates why this might have been the case.

The first incident was the famous condemnation of the ceremonies of the *compagnons du devoir* pronounced by the Faculty of Theology of the Sorbonne in 1655.[21] The doctors of the university were concerned by the blasphemous implications of the initiatory oaths sworn by journeymen when they became *compagnons du devoir*. They singled out journeymen in five trades—harnessmakers, shoemakers, tailors,

20. See above, p. 134.
21. The major texts are reprinted by Coornaert, *Compagnonnages*, 350–56, 415–24.

cutlers, and hatters—for practicing such initiatory ceremonies and condemned them as heretical. The significance of the condemnation lies in the fact that, although the ceremonies proscribed varied from trade to trade (those practiced by the hatters were the most elaborate), journeymen of all trades were initiated into the same association. The *compagnons du devoir* were not, in other words, trade-specific. The occupations of the victims of the attack on the Mouton Couronné are a confirmation of this fact. Although some of them were journeymen hatters, the others were curriers, tanners, and joiners. The inn was also used by journeymen carpenters who were *compagnons du devoir*. Further evidence can be found in an episode that occurred in the small town of Auxerre in 1760. Early in June of that year, two Parisian journeymen locksmiths were assaulted by the local *compagnons du devoir*.[22] Their assailants included two journeymen hatters, a journeyman locksmith, a file cutter (*tailleur de limes*), and two journeymen joiners.

These episodes present an image of the *compagnons du devoir* that is somewhat at variance with the notion of an association of highly skilled journeymen setting out on a *Tour de France* to master the intricacies of their trade. Instead, it appears as an association that was not trade-specific because it catered to the needs of migrants. Its characteristic institution was the *cayenne*, or house of call, with its *mère* and *rouleur*, who were able to supply a bed, a meal, and a job. It met the most elementary needs of young men on the margins of a trade, journeymen from small towns in search of more stable and prosperous employment who did not have the resources provided by relatively permanent residence in a big city.

In the hatting trade of the big cities—in Paris, Lyon, and Marseille—the *compagnons du devoir* were a minority. The evidence from Lyon and Marseille is confirmed by evidence from Paris. No trace of the *compagnons du devoir* can be found

22. A.D. Yonne, 1B 579 (11 June 1760). More generally, see Sonenscher, "Mythical Work."

between 1655, when the Sorbonne condemned the ceremonies of the journeymen hatters, and the last quarter of the eighteenth century.[23] Indications of their presence in the capital begin to appear only after 1776 and the reorganization of the corporations of that year. In 1783 there was a fight in an inn called the Chapeau Rouge between four journeymen hatters and a group of a dozen other journeymen who also worked in the trade and were attached to the *devoir*.[24] In June 1789 a hatter named Danloux-Dumesnil on the rue Saint-Denis complained that twenty-four of his journeymen calling themselves *les bons enfants* had refused to work alongside twenty-two *compagnons du devoir*. When Dumesnil rejected their demand to dismiss the members of the *devoir* because, he said, he was not prepared to sacrifice twenty-two reliable workers, the *bons enfants* walked out. They went to several *fabriques* to enlist support and held a number of meetings. Some of Dumesnil's other workers were persuaded to join them and were paid 45 sous a day while they were out. An *approprieur* described how he had been paid in a *cabaret* on the rue Sainte-Avoye by an elderly journeyman hatter, whose face was scarred by smallpox, for stopping work for four days.[25]

Again the impression is of a division between journeymen domiciled in Paris, with their own established practices (the *bons enfants*), and journeymen on the margins of the trade who were viewed, at least by one employer, as more reliable and conscientious. A police report of 1807 confirms the balance of forces. It stated that all over France journeymen in the hatting trade were divided into two associations known as the *bons enfants* and the *compagnons du devoir*. In Paris there were about eight hundred journeymen affiliated to the former association and some sixty *compagnons du devoir*. The *bons enfants* made use of their numerical superiority

23. This appears to be the case generally: see Garrioch and Sonenscher, "Compagnonnages, Confraternities, and Journeymen's Associations."
24. A.N. Y 11 978 (28 January 1783).
25. A.N. Y 13 016ᵃ (12 June 1789).

to prevent members of the *devoir* from working in the capital.[26]

It has been said that journeymen's associations in the eighteenth century were modified forms of masters' corporations.[27] In the light of what has been presented here, it would seem that the reality was more complex and that the *compagnonnages* were more varied in their identity. It may be more accurate to characterize the *compagnons du devoir*, in particular, as counter-confraternities, which borrowed and modified the ceremonial of recognized journeymen's confraternities. It is possible, although there is no evidence to support the claim, that their appearance in the hatting trade complemented the recognition given to journeymen's confraternities in the latter half of the seventeenth century. For it should not be forgotten that there was a long period during which established journeymen's associations enjoyed a relatively well-defined place in public life. The confraternity of journeymen hatters in Paris was recognized by the *lieutenant-général de police* in 1673 and was granted two papal bulls. Its counterpart in Marseille continued its public existence until the last years of the Old Regime. Only in Lyon is there no trace of official recognition of a journeymen's association other than for a brief period after 1744. It is easier to understand the journeymen's persistent recourse to the courts in the light of this situation. It is also easier to understand the relative success of the Parisian journeymen's campaigns against the journeymen known as *compagnons battans la semelle* in the late seventeenth and early eighteenth centuries. And it may not be too extravagant to suggest that *compagnons battans la semelle* and *compagnons du devoir* were journeymen in similar circumstances: single men who prob-

26. "Les garçons chapeliers sont divisés dans presque toute la France en deux associations connues sous la dénomination de compagnons de *bons enfants* et de *compagnons du devoir*. Les premiers s'autorisent de leur nombre pour empêcher les autres d'être reçues dans les atteliers de la capitale." A.N. F⁷ 3757 (1 October 1807).

27. Sewell, *Work and Revolution*, 58–61. Again, my interpretation is not incompatible with Sewell's discussion but implies a broader range of associational forms.

ably learned their trade in small towns and were able to find work most easily in the suburbs and on the fringes of established workplaces; men who were most vulnerable to collective pressure from journeymen who had served their apprenticeship or settled successfully in one of the three principal centers of the hatting trade.

This does not mean that the journeymen's associations that were dominant in Paris, Lyon, and Marseille did not share some of the rituals associated with the *compagnons du devoir*. During the dispute of the summer of 1748, the Parisian hatters complained of the amount of drinking that took place when journeymen left or were placed in a new shop. The practice consisted of drinking as many pints of wine as there were workers in a workshop. According to the master hatters, it resulted in a great deal of lost time and happened far too often.[28] Rituals like this one or the wager between champions of the rival journeymen's associations that led to the previously mentioned fight in the Chapeau Rouge had their place in the everyday life of workshop production. It would be naive to imagine a sharp distinction between young, single migrants on the one hand and settled, married men on the other. In normal circumstances they coexisted and cooperated. This, one suspects, was what such rituals allowed them to do. Yet the rules of the journeymen's associations of Paris, Lyon, and Marseille—with their regular weekly collections, their relatively substantial and prolonged payments to the ill or the infirm, and their provision for old age—make it clear that they embodied the concerns of men who did not need the services of a *mère* or a *rouleur*.[29] These men worked and lived for long periods, if not for the same employer, at least in the same place.

28. "Ce privilège qu'ils veulent s'attribuer de se placer les uns les autres occasionne un découragement considérable appellé *devoir*, qui consiste à boire autant de pintes de vin qu'il y a d'ouvriers dans chaque boutique, ce qui les empêche de travailler plusieurs jours et ce qui leur arrive fort souvent." Archives de la Préfecture de police, Fonds Lamoignon 38, fol. 436 (31 July 1748).

29. For these rules, see above, chapter 7.

The pitched battles and litigation between *droguins, bons enfants, gavots,* and *compagnons du devoir* in the last quarter of the eighteenth century were indicative of the gradual destruction of the distinctive bastion of legal rights that separated journeymen who worked in Paris, Lyon, and Marseille from those who lived and worked elsewhere. As both the materials used to make hats and the status of those who made them came to have more in common with their equivalents in Bourges or Tours, Mâcon or Nîmes, and scores of other localities where hats were made for local consumption, tensions among journeymen became more evident. At the same time, however, the changes that had occurred in the trade continued to generate conflict between journeymen and their masters. The last decade of the Old Regime was one of almost unremitting litigation punctuated by intermittent stoppages.

12

The End of Legal Privilege

The state of relations in the trade was reflected in a manuscript produced in 1781 by one of the officials (*gardes*) of the hatters' corporation of Lyon, named Jacques Buisson. The work, which was presented in the form of an open letter, contained a deeply pessimistic account of the prevailing atmosphere in the trade and an elaborate proposal for its reorganization, modeled upon the structure of the Grande Fabrique, the city's great silk industry.[1] According to Buisson, the letter had been written out of the experience of an infinity of revolts by workers in the trade during the past twenty years. Nor had these revolts abated. In April 1780 there had been a stoppage by journeymen working on the finishing side of the trade. Women who worked as *éplucheuses, cardeuses,* and *coupeuses* had also formed combinations. Recently there had been a terrible combination (*une cabale terrible*) by women working in one enterprise. Its reverberations had been slight only because the women had won all their demands.[2]

In Buisson's eyes the conflicts were a result of the size of the manufactories and the large concentrations of workers to which they gave rise. Between twenty and a hundred workers piled (*entassés*) into a single establishment were, he wrote, the source of all the storms that had occurred in the

1. B.M. Lyon, MS. 11 4107, "Lettre de M. Buisson à MM les maîtres gardes et députés du corps des maîtres et marchands chapeliers de la ville de Lyon" (1781). In December 1781 Buisson resigned his office for reasons that are not recorded (A.D. Rhône, 3E 5110 [300] [12 December 1781]).

2. "Récemment une cabale terrible s'est élevée parmi elles dans une des fabriques, et si elle n'a pas eu des suites dangereuses, c'est qu'elles ont obtenu les injustices qu'elles demandoient." Ibid. I have not been able to find any other record of these events.

hatting trade. The solution, he suggested, was to create a system of production analogous to that of the Grande Fabrique, with its four tiers of *marchands fabricants, maîtres marchands, maîtres ouvriers,* and *compagnons* working in small, dispersed workshops. He proposed that journeymen working on the felting side of the trade should be given the opportunity to become master workers (*maîtres ouvriers*) and set themselves up in their own small workshops with no more than six or eight *compagnons.* Those employed on the finishing side of the trade should, as far as possible, be distributed in small groups outside the manufactories, preferably working at home and never on a daily rate. A multitude of small workshops would replace the large manufactories in which so many different kinds of people were crowded together.[3]

If this "proto-industrial" solution to the problems of the hatting trade was one person's idea of the shape of things to come, conditions in the trade continued to echo the enduring concerns of the journeymen themselves. As Buisson observed with bewildered irritation, workers on the felting side of the trade in Lyon continued to maintain a limit on the number of hats they were prepared to make in a week. Journeymen in Marseille and Paris did likewise. What a journeyman in Marseille had termed *le règlement de Paris* continued to be practiced in the capital. An enterprising manufacturer named Joseph Lacoste, who engaged a dozen journeymen to leave Paris early in 1785 to set up a hatting concern in the state of New York, found it necessary to insert a clause in their agreement stipulating that each journeyman had undertaken to produce at least twelve hats a week.[4]

The cycle of disputes that took place during the last decade of the Old Regime was marked both by the continuity

3. "Une multitude de petits ateliers remplacerait des établissements où sont entassés tant d'êtres de toutes espèces." Ibid.
4. "Les compagnons seront tenus, ainsi qu'ils s'y obligent personnellement de fournir chacun douze chapeaux par semaine au moins." A.N. Minutier central, CXIX 480 (11 January 1785).

of such attitudes and practices and by the deepening erosion of what formal legal status they once had had. Although there were disputes in Paris in 1781 and 1782, it was again the end of a war (the American War of Independence) and the subsequent revival of international trade that appears to have contributed most to the broad campaign by journeymen that developed from 1784 onward.[5]

In every locality relations between established journeymen's associations and the *compagnons du devoir* had become increasingly strained. The journeymen of Marseille were involved in legal proceedings with the *devoirants* but had been denied the right to meet to raise the extra money needed for their action. Early in January 1784, following their consultation with a barrister in Aix, they presented a twenty-two–page memorandum to the Parlement of Provence requesting the right to assemble. As their legal adviser had recommended, they made no mention of the immediate purpose of the proposed assembly. Instead they concentrated upon the wholly acceptable charitable functions of the Luminaire de Sainte-Catherine de Sienne. The memorandum emphasized the increasing penury of its members, many of whom were married with dependents, and reiterated the grave (and costly) effects of the use of the *eau de composition* in the production of hats. The journeymen complained that they had been systematically victimized by the masters' corporation, whose members, they said flamboyantly, carried a germ of hatred toward their workers in their hearts and had been their sworn enemies at all times.[6] The charge was widened to include the municipal authorities, whose officials, the journeymen stated, had invariably taken pleasure in refusing whatever the workers in the hatting trade—or any

---

5. It has not been possible to find any trace of the two disputes in 1781 and 1782. They are mentioned by Coornaert, *Compagnonnages*, 426, but no source is cited.

6. "Les maîtres fabricants de chapeaux ont été de tous les tems les ennemis jurés de leurs ouvriers. . . . Les maîtres gardent toujours dans leur coeur un espèce de levain de la haine qu'ils ont portée de tous les tems aux ouvriers." A.C. Marseille, HH 399.

other trade—had sought to obtain. It was evident, they concluded, that the *échevins* had been prejudiced against them by the master hatters.[7]

This attempt seems to have been the last by the journeymen in Marseille to obtain the sanction of the law for their association. There is no sign that the Parlement responded favorably to their memorandum, and it is very likely that the magistrates were well aware of the tension between different journeymen's associations that was the real, but unstated, reason for the petition. In the face of this silence, the journeymen adopted their own sanctions. In June 1784 a small number of them walked out of a workshop where a *compagnon du devoir* had been engaged.[8] There were brawls between members of the rival associations.[9] Consequently, what appears to have been a concerted campaign by journeymen in all three cities to improve wage rates and working conditions in 1785 was, in Marseille more than in Lyon or Paris, deeply affected by the continuing antagonism between different groups of journeymen.

The first indication of the campaign was a request presented by thirty-five Parisian journeymen (presumably the delegates of that number of *fabriques*) to the Parlement of Paris in April 1785.[10] It took the form of an appeal against a ruling by the *lieutenant général de police*, Lenoir, in January of that year fixing the range of rates for making fourteen different types of hats. The journeymen called upon the Parlement to order the master hatters to continue to pay the previous rates. The types of hats specified in the petition make it clear that the hatting trade in Paris had also largely

7. "De tous les tems les lieutenants de police de Marseille ce sont faits un plaisir de refuser ce que les garçons chapelliers, et tous les autres ouvriers de quelque art de métier, demandent. . . . Les maîtres fabricans quelconques lui [*sic*] fassent regarder les ouvriers de mauvais oeil." Ibid.

8. A.C. Marseille, FF 394 (1 July 1784).

9. A.D. Bouches-du-Rhône, B 5653 (9 September 1784), *arrêt* upholding a sentence of the *échevins* of Marseille of 13 August 1784 and referring to an earlier sentence of 11 December 1783. The earlier sentence probably precipitated the litigation between the two associations of journeymen.

10. A.N. X^{1b} 4232 (28 April 1785).

ceased to produce hats made of beaver fur. Instead, hats were made of a variety of materials, in which the fur of bears (*oursons*) was most usual. The rates that the journeymen demanded were lower than those that had been set in 1751 for the highest quality beaver hats and ranged from 3 livres 10 sous for what were termed black and white plumed hats (*chapeaux à plumet blanc sur noir*) and bearskin hats (*chapeaux ourson*), to 1 livre 5 sous and 2 livres for other types of bear fur hats (*chapeaux pluché*, i.e., *peluché*).[11] Significantly, the journeymen also specified that an extra 10 sous should be added to the rates if they were required to make hats from the fur of hares.

In June the Parlement issued its verdict. In an oblique reference to the vexed matter of the number of hats made in a day, it accepted the masters' claim that they had never sought anything else than to pay their journeymen rates that were in keeping with the amount of work that they did. The court dismissed the journeymen's case and condemned them to pay the costs.[12]

At the same time that this case was under way in Paris, a serious dispute was beginning in Marseille. Early in May 1785 eighty journeymen employed by a manufacturer named Pierre Mazières abandoned his *fabrique*. He had refused to accept their demand for an increase in their rates from some 15 to 20 sous a hat. Mazières brought the dispute before the corporation, complaining that many of his employees had been taken on by other manufacturers at the higher rate. The corporation agreed to support him, but only with considera-

11. The full range of hats consisted of *oursons*, 3 livres 5 sous; *demi-oursons*, 3 livres; *chapeau à plumet avec bordure dessous*, 3 livres; *chapeau à plumet simple*, 2 livres 10 sous; *chapeau à plumet blanc sur noir*, 3 livres 10 sous; *chapeau peluché, à poil d'une once*, 2 livres; *chapeau peluché, à poil d'une demie-once*, 1 livre 10 sous; *joquey ourson*, 2 livres 10 sous; *demi-ourson*, 2 livres 10 sous; *demi-ourson avec bordure doublé, sans cordon*, 2 livres 10 sous; *demi-ourson à plumet simple*, 2 livres; *demi-ourson peluché à poil, doré d'une once*, 1 livre 10 sous; *demi-ourson à poil, doré d'une demie-once*, 1 livre 5 sous (A.N. X^{1b} 4232 [28 April 1785]).

12. "Ils n'avoient jamais mieux demandé que de payer leurs compagnons conformément à leur travail." A.N. X^{1b} 8727 (9 May 1785); X^{1b} 4236 (22 June 1785).

ble misgivings: nineteen of the forty-two masters present at the assembly refused to sign the minute recording their decision.[13]

By then, the conflict had spread to a number of other workshops. In June 1785 all the journeymen employed by a manufacturer named Rancurel, including his own brother and brother-in-law, walked out.[14] The journeymen placed an embargo of a year and a day on his establishment. Similar actions were repeated over the ensuing weeks. The journeymen were no longer able, however, to extend their action to the trade as a whole. Much of their time appears to have been devoted to attempting to persuade or coerce other journeymen to refuse to work for blacklisted employers. In October 1785 the corporation decided to obtain a ruling from the municipal authorities on the scale of piece rates.[15] It was not until February 1786, however, that it made a formal complaint against the journeymen and drew the *échevins* into the dispute.

The hearings were conducted in a leisurely way. They began on 24 February but were not concluded (although only eighteen witnesses were called) until 3 May 1786.[16] They revealed substantial divisions among the journeymen. Six individuals summoned to give evidence reported that they knew nothing of the stoppages and embargoes organized by the confraternity. Three others who had remained at work and whose names—Noble Coeur le Percheron, Saint-Amour de Bergerac, and La Réjouissance d'Amboise— are evocative of the sobriquets of the *compagnons du devoir* described how they had been subjected to levies of 2 or 3 livres before they were allowed to work in Marseille. They had been threatened with even more intimidating fines if they worked for prohibited employers. The tenor of the pro-

13. A.D. Bouches-du Rhône, 367E²⁷⁹, fol. 883 (24 May 1785); ibid., C 3399; A.C. Marseille, FF 204 (15 June 1785); A.N. F¹² 1461.
14. Details of the sequence of events have been reconstructed from A.C. Marseille, FF 396.
15. A.D. Bouches-du-Rhône, 367E²⁸⁰, fol. 1563v (5 October 1785).
16. A.C. Marseille, FF 396.

ceedings was very different from those of 1761 and 1774. Only one person referred openly to the charitable purpose of the journeymen's confraternity.[17] Others denied all knowledge of its existence. Still others reported incidents involving the payment of fines by newcomers or stoppages by journeymen already at work who refused to accept the presence of new arrivals. When the hearings were over, the court ordered the arrest of a dozen journeymen. Only six could be found. They maintained a complete silence on the charges made against them.

The sporadic stoppages and boycotts of selected manufacturers continued, however, to take place. In May 1786, a *fabricant* who had been deprived of journeymen issued a summons on the corporation ordering it to revive the corporate labor exchange (*bureau de placement*) that had been established in 1774 but had collapsed ignominiously soon afterward. The corporation noted bitterly that plots and combinations by workers in the trade had reached such a level that the revival of a corporate labor exchange would be incapable of containing them.[18] The only solution, it stated, to the desertions, combinations, plots, and disruptive activities fomented by the journeymen would be full-scale civil and criminal proceedings. Workers in the hatting trade were, it claimed, better paid than ever before. The stoppages and disruption upon which they had embarked had been provoked by the malevolence of their leaders, whose aim, the corporation stated extravagantly, was to annihilate the trade altogether.[19]

One further solution, raised and rejected in April but finally approved in October, was to allow the victims of boy-

17. Ibid., deposition of Félix Jaume.
18. "Les complots journaliers et continus des ouvriers étant portés à leur comble, l'établissement d'un embaucheur ne pourra jamais être capable de les contenir." A.D. Bouches-du-Rhône, 367E²⁵¹, fol. 682 (16 May 1786).
19. "Ils sont payés à un prix plus fort qu'ils n'aient jamais été. . . . Leurs desordres et leurs désertions survient de l'esprit de tracasserie et de méchanceté de ceux à qui ils se laissent diriger, qui trouvent non seulement un intérêt à les desunir des maîtres, mais encore une satisfaction à anéantir s'ils pourraient les fabriques et la fabrication." Ibid.

cotts to sublet their premises and work out to other masters. Article 28 of the corporate statutes prohibited anyone from leasing equipment to a master who did not also own a vat for felting hats. Its purpose was to limit the scale of subcontracted work and prevent too great a concentration of the means of production among large manufacturers. In October 1786, by a majority of only twenty-two to nineteen, the corporation accepted a proposal allowing any of its members with the appropriate installations the right to lease places to whomever they wished.[20]

The process of disassociating working conditions from the law was by now almost complete. Yet such matters were not now left to individual negotiation. Journeymen continued to press their claims in the courts and, in one brief period, they enjoyed a limited degree of success. This occurred in the best known of the episodes in this cycle of conflict, which took place in Lyon and intersected with the famous *révolte des deux sous* of the city's silk weavers in August 1786.[21] By then, however, the dispute in the hatting trade had been under way for several months. Although the journeymen in Lyon were able to take advantage of the temporary disarray of the authorities that occurred in August 1786, their movement was an extension of the campaign that had developed in Paris and Marseille in 1785.

The movement developed as a counterpoint to the revival of the trade after the end of the war. During 1785 there were a series of disputes in which the aim of the journeymen on both the felting and finishing sides of the trade appears to have been to bring their wages into line with those in Paris.[22] Two large employers—each with over sixty workers—were selected as the objects of the campaign. A third was the recipient of an anonymous letter calling upon him to agree to a new

20. "Chaque membre qui a les fonds a la permission de louer des places à qui bon leur semble." A.D. Bouches-du-Rhône, 367E²⁸¹, fol. 509v (3 April 1786); ibid., fol. 593v (2 May 1786); 367E²⁸², fol. 1469 (17 October 1786).
21. See Louis Trénard, "La Crise sociale lyonnaise à la veille de la Révolution," *Revue d'histoire moderne et contemporaine*, n.s. 2 (1955): 5–45.
22. A.N. F¹² 1441, "Mémoire des maîtres chapeliers" (7 August 1786).

set of rates and to hire a servant to carry out work such as lighting fires for vats and carrying wood, coal, or wine residue, for which journeymen were not paid.[23] In the face of this campaign, the corporation abandoned its previous commitment to free contractual arrangements between individuals and invoked the rates set by the Parlement of Paris in 1762. On 13 December 1785 it obtained an ordinance from the Consulat reaffirming the general terms of the *arrêt*, although the rates for two sorts of hats were raised. It was also empowered by the authorities to revise its statutes in the light of current conditions in the trade.

On 27 December 1785 there was a general assembly of journeymen representing all branches of the trade. Some 210 people from thirty-three *fabriques* gathered at an inn called the Luxembourg, where they decided to appeal to the Parlement against the ordinance. They elected four deputies, two in Lyon and two in Paris, to take charge of the proceedings. They also declared their opposition to any modification of the statutes before their own opinion had been heard.[24]

The case appears to have followed a slow itinerary through the Parlement during the ensuing months. In the late summer of 1786, matters came to a head during a concatenation of disputes in a variety of trades, of which the most substantial concerned the silk weavers. On 4 August the hatters' corporation met to hear a report on the progress of the legal proceedings.[25] They were informed that the journeymen on the finishing side of the trade had presented a request to the Parlement demanding that masters should be allowed only one apprentice at a time, that workers should be prohibited from working at home or on subcontracted work, that *approprieurs* should receive a daily rate of 40 sous as they did in Paris, and that two weeks' notice should be obligatory before any worker could be dismissed.

23. Ibid.
24. A.D. Rhône, 3E 4381 (27 December 1785).
25. Ibid., 3E 9731 (223) (4 August 1786).

The report raised some anxiety. The journeymen's deputies had apparently had a sympathetic hearing. They had besieged the magistrates of the Parlement with the case, and, the corporation noted, it was to be feared that they would be successful. The corporation decided to send its own representative to the capital, particularly because it feared that the journeymen had won the support of master hatters in Paris, who, according to the hatters of Lyon, were ever prepared to encourage journeymen outside Paris to campaign for higher wages in order to eliminate competition from their lower-priced articles.[26]

Events ran ahead of their fears. On 8 August, while the *gardes* of the corporation were finishing the final draft of a memorandum to the *contrôleur général des finances* on the proceedings against the journeymen, the *approprieurs* walked out. On the following day the Consulat, already overwhelmed by the silk weavers' revolt, received a deputation from the journeymen and agreed to raise their daily rate from 32 sous 6 deniers to 40 sous. The journeymen returned to work that evening.[27] On 11 August the masters assembled again and decided that, once order had been restored in the city, they would appeal against the increase. They noted that the old daily rate of 32 sous 6 deniers was, in real terms, higher than the 40 sous a day paid in Paris, given the difference in prices and the kind of work that the journeymen did.[28] On the following day, with a speed that was characteristic of the authorities in moments of crisis, two *approprieurs* were executed for their part in the revolt.[29]

---

26. "Ils obsèdent, ils assiègent nos seigneurs du Parlement, et leurs sollicitations font craindre avec fondement qu'ils obtiennent ce qu'ils ont l'injustice de demander." Parisian hatters "ont intérêt de faire augmenter les salaires à Lyon, parce qu'il sera alors impossible aux maîtres et marchands de cette ville de donner leurs marchandises à bas prix." Ibid.

27. B.N. MS. Joly de Fleury 560, fol. 279.

28. "La journée qu'ils payent sur le pied de 32 sols et demi est plus forte que celle de 40 sols à Paris, comparaison faitte de la qualité des ouvrages, de la quantité de travail et du prix des denrées." A.D. Rhône, 3E 5115 (176) (11 August 1786).

29. A.D. Rhône, BP 3510. Five others were arrested and later pardoned.

Moves to reverse the capitulation followed rapidly. The corporation's appeal against the ordinance of 9 August 1786 was duly presented to the Parlement.[30] Early in September the Conseil du roi issued an edict abolishing all piece-rate scales in the silk industry. The hatters decided to use the decision as a justification for the abolition of a fixed daily rate on the finishing side of the trade. On 18 September some 250 *approprieurs* stopped work.[31] The stoppage continued for two weeks, until the arrest of four of the journeymen resulted in a gradual drift back to work. By the end of September all but a dozen had returned.[32] Some months later the corporation presented a draft of its revised statutes. Its terms underlined the scale of the masters' objectives. They were to be entitled to employ as many men and women as they deemed necessary, either inside or outside their workshops and on whatever conditions they chose, whether by the day, by the piece, on subcontracted work, or otherwise.[33] The remaining revisions were an elaboration of this general principle. They amounted to the formal annihilation of the distinctive practices and recognized legal rights that had once informed conditions of work.

Too much should not, however, be made of a draft. Its significance lies less in its (probably limited) effects upon the reality of working conditions than in the transformation of the formal status of journeymen that it signified. It represented a redefinition of the relationship between the public and the private so that the vocabulary of the law no longer qualified or transcended arrangements made in a purely contractual sense between individuals. The normative vocabulary of the tradition of natural law was no longer a grid demarcating the qualities of particular kinds of work or the

30. A.N. X[1b] 8762 (2 September 1786).
31. A.N. F[12] 1441.
32. Ibid., Terray to Calonne (23 and 29 September 1786).
33. "Tel nombre d'ouvriers et ouvrières qui leur sera nécessaire, tant dans leurs ateliers que dehors, et sous telle dénomination que ce puisse être, soit à journée, soit à prix fait, à pieces ou à façon." A.N. F[12] 763, "Projet de statuts" (1787).

distinctive attributes of those who carried it out. Its precepts were consigned to folklore.

There are no further signs that the journeymen in Lyon pursued their objectives in the courts. In Marseille too the breach between journeymen and the law appears to have become complete. Throughout 1786 and 1787 there were isolated stoppages and repeated fights between journeymen and the *compagnons du devoir*. In May 1787 the corporation of Marseille recorded that it had received complaints from several of its members arising from the total desertion of their workshops by their workers.[34] The walkouts were accompanied by serious riots in the city as members of rival journeymen's associations fought pitched battles on the streets of Marseille. On 22 May the Parlement issued an *arrêt* ordering the lower courts to transfer proceedings arising from these incidents to itself.[35] A day later it issued a general condemnation of all journeymen's associations and, on 21 June, produced an *arrêt de règlement* abolishing the Luminaire de Sainte-Catherine de Sienne.[36] On the last day of June, the papers of the confraternity were seized in the convent of the order of Recollets where they had been deposited for the past twenty years.[37]

The *arrêt* ended the long, occasionally tenuous, formal recognition enjoyed by the journeymen's confraternity in Marseille. Stoppages continued. Early in 1788 the corporation decided to set a new series of rates because, it said, the license of workers in the trade had reached new heights.[38] A large number of journeymen appear to have left Marseille. In February 1788 the hatters' corporation was sued by one of

34. "Ils ont reçu ces jours derniers des plaintes de la part de divers membres du corps de la désertion totale de leurs fabriques par leurs ouvriers, et que bien d'autres membres et presque tous ont vu également déserter leurs fabriques." A.D. Bouches-du-Rhône, 367E²⁸³, fol. 707v (23 May 1787).

35. Ibid., B 5656 (22 May 1787).

36. Ibid., B 5656 (23 May 1787); B 3707 (21 June 1787).

37. A.C. Marseille, FF 397 (30 June 1787).

38. "D'autant que la licence des ouvriers est aujourd'hui à son comble." A.D. Bouches-du-Rhône, 367E²⁸⁵, fol. 61 (18 January 1788).

its revenue collectors, who demanded a reduction of a third on the sum of 900 livres that he had agreed to pay for the right to collect a sou a week from every member of the trade. He claimed that since he had signed the agreement, the number of journeymen in the city had fallen considerably and, as a result, revenue from the levy was very much lower. The conduct of the masters toward their workers was, he said, the cause of his losses.[39] Despite or perhaps because of the continuing refusal of journeymen to work in Marseille, the corporation recovered some of its authority. At the end of February, it decided to establish a *bureau de placement* for the journeymen.[40] The resuscitation of this much derided and notably unsuccessful institution was indicative of the change in the balance of forces. As the assembly that made the decision came to an end, a dissenting voice was heard to observe that the masters themselves had also formed *cabales*.[41]

It was, of course, true that they had. So too had the journeymen. The long series of disputes in which both had been involved had considerably changed the environment in which they worked. The distinctive claims of journeymen in Paris, Lyon, and Marseille to determine with whom they worked, how they worked, and how they should be paid—claims that both echoed and were echoed by the prescriptions of the law—were by the last decade of the Old Regime no longer part of the discourse and practice of either corporate statutes or the courts themselves. It was therefore fitting that the epigraph attached by the Genevan doctor Gosse to his essay on the means to prevent workers in the hatting trade from suffering from the effects of the *eau de composition* should, as Rousseau proclaimed, equate the principle of justice with the love of humanity. The elaborate nexus of proscription and prescription that had formed part of the texture of everyday activity in the hatting trade belonged to

39. "C'est par la conduite des maîtres envers les ouvriers qu'il éprouve la perte dont il se plaint." Ibid., fol. 163v (12 February 1788).
40. Ibid., 367E²⁸⁵, fol. 215v (29 February 1788).
41. "Les maîtres eux-mêmes cabalaient." Ibid.

another order of discourse. The specific claims of the members of a particular trade were displaced by the simpler claims of humanity. Instead of the limited and exceptional rights that were the possession of particular individuals or collectivities, rights and obligations were defined in a more universal way. This, in turn, implied a different relationship between individuals and the collectivity and between the private and the public spheres. Rights were no longer titles of an exceptional kind. They were common to the collectivity as a whole.

Conclusion:
Patterns of Work and
Journeymen's Politics

The revolutionary crisis resulted in a recovery of some of this lost terrain. In the spring of 1789, journeymen in the hatting trade elected their own delegates to assemblies of the Third Estate and drew up their own lists of grievances in ways that echoed the procedures they had followed in addressing the courts during the eighteenth century. The continuities of form are significant. Historians have devoted much time to the problem of the content of the *cahiers de doléances* and, having discovered that they have little to say about liberty, equality, or any of the great themes of revolutionary politics, have concluded that they are best treated as a kind of proto–Gallup poll in which most of the respondents appear to have had a rather blinkered interest in parochial affairs.[1] It is necessary to emphasize that, on the contrary, this concern with the parochial was also a claim upon the public sphere, a reassertion of a mode of dialogue with the law and the courts that had become an anachronism. When journeymen hatters met to contribute to the forthcoming assembly of the Estates General, they recovered a public identity of which they had been divested by the law in the space of little more than a generation.

The men they chose as their deputies were symbols of their awareness of the situation. In Marseille they chose

---

1. See for example, George V. Taylor, "Revolutionary and Nonrevolutionary Content in the *Cahiers* of 1789: An Interim Report," *French Historical Studies* 7 (1972): 479–502.

Jean-François Chaussegros, who had been served with a warrant for his arrest after the dispute in 1785.[2] In their *cahier* they called for the reestablishment of the Luminaire de Sainte-Catherine de Sienne, whose existence, they said, had been authorized and confirmed by the *arrêt* of the Parlement of Provence of 20 February 1764.[3] In Lyon one of the deputies chosen by the journeymen was Jean-Pierre Simard, whose difficulties with the masters' corporation went back to 1770.[4] No trace of any similar choice exists for Paris, where the *cahiers* of the corporations have disappeared. Perhaps an undated printed *tarif* drawn up by the master hatters of the capital at some time after 1790 in response, it said, to the workers' exorbitant demands for an increase in wages, and still denominated in livres, sous, and deniers, tells its own story.[5]

The history of the trade during and after the Revolution falls beyond the scope of this essay. Other circumstances— the abolition of the corporations, the effects of production for war upon the organization of work, the immense reorganization of circuits of international trade between 1792 and 1815— affected the environment in which that history occurred. The brief reenactment of the procedures of eighteenth-century litigation in the initial phase of the Revolution was followed by a mode of political transaction that owed much to informal relations between masters and journeymen and found its expression in the metaphor of the sans-culotte.[6] The consolidation of institutional stability after 1794 was accompanied by the elaboration of a codified system of legal procedure. By the early nineteenth century, the tradition of natural law had been displaced by the positive law of the Civil Code and the rulings of the courts.

---

2. A.C. Marseille, FF 396; A.D. Bouches-du-Rhône, 358E²²⁵, fol. 197v (24 March 1789).

3. Joseph Fournier, *Cahiers de doléances de la sénéchaussée de Marseille* (Marseille, 1908), 72.

4. A.D. Rhône, 3E 9734 (73) (27 February 1789).

5. A.N. F¹² 1461.

6. Sonenscher, "The Sans-Culottes of the Year II."

There were, however, continuities. As we have seen, hatters in Lyon (and presumably in Paris) continued to limit the number of hats that they were prepared to make to two a day.[7] The evidence does not suggest that they did so because they could earn enough on a limited output to make additional work unnecessary. Piece rates do not seem to have risen by much more than the average rate of wage increases during the eighteenth century. In 1726 the rate for a nine- to twelve-ounce brown or white beaver hat in Paris was set at 35 sous. The scale of rates drawn up by the Parisian hatters after 1790 set a figure of 45 sous for a nine- to ten-ounce black and white beaver hat: an increase of 10 sous (28.5 percent) over more than sixty years.[8] The composition and weights of the hats in question are not entirely comparable, so that no precise estimate of the trend can be established. This, together with short-term deviations from notionally uniform rates (as well as the vexed question of how many of up to fourteen different types of hats a journeyman might have made) means that it is impossible to translate piece rates into real earnings. Yet even a limited comparison between piece rates suggests that the maximum of two hats a day was maintained for reasons other than high levels of earnings, stable levels of consumption, and a resultant capacity to limit working time. It derived instead from the working arrangements established by the pairs of journeymen employed on the felting side of the trade.

By the early nineteenth century a practice that had once enjoyed the sanction of the law and had been the subject of protracted debate in the courts had become an informal custom. It is tempting to describe this process in linear terms and reverse an established developmental image of historical change centered upon the notion of modernization. For what happened in the eighteenth-century French hatting trade was a transition from legal rights to informal customs,

7. See above, chapter 3.
8. B.N. F 26429 (6 September 1726); A.N. Y 9498 (30 August 1726); ibid., F[12] 1461.

rather than the reverse. Yet even that interpretation remains
a simplification. For the Revolution did not end the dialogue
between the law and the trades. In the hatting trade, municipal authorities continued to set scales of piece rates in
the early nineteenth century, even though they were incompatible with the "true principles of political economy."[9] In
different ways and in different contexts, the law remained
one of the components of the wider environment of industrial relations in which the history of labor in France took
place. As far as the work of making hats was concerned,
what changed were the terms of reference and mode of relationship between the law and the trade.

For much of the eighteenth century, however, the prevailing conventions of civil jurisprudence allowed journeymen
in the hatting trade considerable scope to present various
aspects of the work of making hats to the adjudication of the
courts. Journeymen in the hatting trade also played an active part in initiating litigation in which issues affecting the
trade as a whole were at the center of legal argument. In
both these respects, it is unlikely that the hatting trade was
unusual. Until the late eighteenth century, the limited and
exceptional character of civil rights meant that claims and
counter-claims could be argued in the courts, even when the
collective identity of journeymen as litigants was itself a
matter of legal argument.[10] Disputes in the hatting trade
were therefore closely related to argument of a legal character. The timing and selectivity of stoppages of work were
frequently designed to force manufacturers in the small core
of large hatting enterprises in Paris, Lyon, or Marseille to
comply with rulings by the courts.

The prevailing conventions of eighteenth-century civil jurisprudence also contained one of the keys to the abiding
commitment of journeymen in the hatting trade to what one

9. See above, chapter 3.
10. For several other examples, see Sonenscher, "Journeymen, the
Courts, and the French Trades," and "Weavers, Wage-Rates, and the Mea-
surement of Work in Eighteenth-Century Rouen," *Textile History* 17 (1986):
7–18.

of them called *le règlement de Paris.* There was no clear economic logic to the journeymen's refusal to make more than two hats a day. All the evidence that can be found indicates that the substitution of hare for beaver fur resulted in higher productivity on the felting side of the trade. The use of hare prepared with the *eau de composition* made it possible to produce a larger number of hats in the same amount of time. In principle, therefore, journeymen were able to earn as much from higher productivity as they had earned before, even if competitive pressures meant that they were paid lower piece rates for producing hats made mainly from hare. This claim was made by master hatters at various times in each of the three cities, and the trial demonstration held in Marseille in 1776 appears to have confirmed their claim. Much, of course, depended upon how low piece rates fell. Yet the journeymen's adherence to the maximum of two hats a day continued to prevail, even when they claimed higher rates for making certain types of hat. It prevailed because they were paid for what they made rather than for what they did. As a result, it was not possible to translate the technical capacity to produce more than two hats a day into a division of labor that could realize that capacity. For the work of making hats followed rules that are intelligible only in the light of a fiction: that journeymen owned the hats they made.

This fiction engendered a pattern of work that was a durable obstacle to any extension of the division of labor. It emerged almost in parenthesis while the four masters and journeymen were engaged in their trial demonstration of hat making in Marseille in 1776. Soon after the trial began the two journeymen objected to the fact that working arrangements were different from those usually followed in the trade. They pointed out that each of the four participants was working alone instead of following the usual practice in a *fabrique* of working in alternating pairs. This practice meant that each journeyman was paid for the hats that he produced while both men made the same number of hats in the course of a week. It also ensured that it was not possible to extend the division of labor to the bowing and fulling phases of the process of making felt because each journeyman was paid solely for the hats that he produced. The wages that journeymen earned were the measure of the goods that they made rather than the time that they spent working.

This distinction was an acknowledgment of the identity of the wage contract as an agreement between proprietors of different kinds. When eighteenth-century jurists discussed the notion of the wage, they did so under the broader rubric of relations between creditors and debtors. They did so because the tradition of natural law implied that journeymen had rights of property in their own labor. The wage was the price paid for the use of that property. As a result, it found its place in works such as Pothier's *Traité du contrat de louage* and was described in such phrases as *le prix d'une journée de travail* or *le prix de la façon d'un chapeau*.[11] This was why journeymen in the hatting trade were paid for what they made rather than for what they did. Although time was a central issue in disputes over the relationship between the composition of various types of hats and the level of piece rates, it was not central to legal argument over working conditions.

The distinction is significant. There is no doubt that the work of making hats in eighteenth-century France entailed a full and carefully measured working week. Journeymen on the felting side of the trade were paid by the piece, but the rates that they were paid bore a close relationship to a precisely measured working day. Many of the disputes of the latter half of the eighteenth century arose from disagreements over how various combinations of different furs would affect the length of time needed to produce a good felt and, consequently, the number of hats that could be made in a day. Even on the finishing side of the trade, where journeymen were paid by the day, master hatters in

11. "Lorsque c'est l'ouvrier qui fournit la matière, c'est un contrat de vente: au contraire, lorsque c'est moi qui fournis à l'ouvrier la matière de l'ouvrage que je lui fais faire, le contrat est un contrat de louage." Pothier, *Traité du contrat de louage*, 352.

Lyon and Paris had no difficulty in producing a precise esti-mate of the amount of work that a journeyman might be expected to complete. If the hatting trade was at all typical, it is very clear that, while periods of employment in a single establishment may have been brief, work in the urban trades of the eighteenth century was neither indifferent to time nor irregular in its rhythms.[12] What mattered in the eighteenth-century French hatting trade was not the nebulous or erratic relationship between free time and working time but the problematic and disputed relationship between paid and un-paid working time.[13] Precisely because the law was silent on this aspect of working conditions, the central issue that di-vided masters and journeymen was the number of hats that could be made in a day. Time mattered in the work of the trades, but in the eighteenth century it did not matter in legal argument about the modalities of that work.

Time mattered in another sense too. There was an initial contradiction between one of the reasons presented by journeymen to justify their refusal to make more than two hats a day and their determination to prevent some indi-viduals from finding work in the trade. In Marseille in 1750 and in Lyon in the early nineteenth century, journeymen stated that the practice of voluntarily limiting the number of hats made in a day would ensure that work would be shared more widely.[14] At the same time, however, they insisted upon preventing journeymen who were not established in the trade from finding employment. Much of the antago-nism between *droguins* and *devoirants* was the result of this

12. For recent work on the question, and a similar argument, see Mark Harrison, "The Ordering of the Urban Environment: Time, Work, and the Occurrence of Crowds, 1790–1835," *Past and Present* 110 (1986): 134–68.

13. According to Nollet, "C'est le maître qui se charge de faire emplir la chaudière, de faire porter de l'eau dans un reservoir pour le remplissage, de faire mettre du bois en suffisante quantité dans quelque endroit qui soit à portée de l'atelier, de fournir la lie et les lumières" (*L'Art de faire des cha-peaux,* 39). Not all masters did so. Even if they did, the additional time that journeymen needed to *prepare* the installations and solutions amounted, on Nollet's own estimate, to approximately a fifth of the working week (see above, chapter 6, n. 15).

14. See above, chapters 3 and 7.

insistence. Work could be shared, but it could not be shared indiscriminately.

The practice of limiting output was thus linked to a perception of membership of the trade that had little to do with aggregate numbers and very much more to do with a calculation of the optimum size of the trade compatible with a given way of life. Journeymen were prepared to deprive some individuals of a living in order to preserve their established sense of the trade. Here, two features of the structure of the trade were particularly significant. In each locality, most master hatters did not produce hats. The majority of journeymen were therefore employed by a relatively small number of master hatters. Labor markets were centered upon a core of large hatting enterprises where large numbers of journeymen were employed. This was the environment in which the apparently contradictory attitudes between making work more widely available on the one hand, and preventing outsiders from finding employment on the other, were established. Continuity of employment within the core of the trade was the prerequisite to opportunities for relatively independent subcontracted work or for repairing and selling hats on the periphery. Time mattered in this context, because the daily and weekly cycles of work, wages, and consumption were bound up with the longer process of accumulating sufficient resources of credit, kin, and patrons to enter the periphery of the trade.

The process of managing the passage of time, both from week to week and over the longer period, endowed journeymen with a sense of the trade that was compatible with a given way of life. This sense was not, of course, pre-given. Everything that we know about the demographic and occupational composition of eighteenth-century French cities indicates that impermanence, instability, and fluidity were as usual in the hatting trade as in many others.[15] Seen as an aggregate of atomized individuals,

15. On geographical mobility in eighteenth-century French towns, see Jean-Claude Perrot, *Genèse d'une ville moderne* 1:153–65; T. J. A. Le Goff,

journeymen in the hatting trade were equally likely to have been immigrants from other localities or local residents, to have been single or married, to have become masters or failed to become masters, to have provided successfully for themselves or disappeared from the trade into the anonymous clientele of the hospitals.[16]

In practice, of course, they were not an aggregate of atomized individuals. The long campaigns in the courts; the costly business of engaging lawyers; the regular meetings, collections, and discussions of legal memoranda; the coordinated stoppages and communication between Paris, Lyon, and Marseille would not have been possible had solidarities and affinities not been created. There were journeymen who recognized *le règlement de Paris* and those who did not. The distinction between them, like the distinction between *droguins* and *devoirants*, was created out of more than pre-given affinities of geographical origin, age, or marital status. It was created by words and gestures that served to define that sense of the trade, which they perceived as compatible with their way of life. It was created in the regular weekly charitable collections, the religious services, processions, funerals and commemorative masses that informed the life of the trade. Most fundamentally, however, it was created in the course of what happened when hats were made.

As they made hats, journeymen were obliged to calculate how they allocated their time between paid and unpaid work. They had to produce a stable balance between individual earnings (measured by the production of a given number of hats) and total working time (consisting of the work involved in unloading materials, lighting fires, preparing felting vats, and delivering and collecting goods). The calculation was the

Vannes and Its Region: A Study of Town and Country in Eighteenth-Century France (London, 1981), 49–58; Jean-Pierre Poussou, *Bordeaux et le sud-ouest au XVIIIe siècle* (Paris, 1983); on the scale of migration in one specific trade, see Sonenscher, "Journeymen's Migrations."

16. For an example, see Colin Jones and Michael Sonenscher, "The Social Function of the Hospital in Eighteenth-Century France: The Case of the Hôtel-Dieu of Nîmes," *French Historical Studies* 13 (1983): 172–214.

more important because, even at its most stable, the work-force in the hatting trade (as in most other trades) was very heterogeneous in its composition.[17] Journeymen worked in pairs, but they were engaged individually. If, as in Marseille, each enterprise had its *goret*, who had been employed for the longest period of time, there were also many other differ-ences in seniority, experience, age, origin, and expectations within its workforce. The title of the association in Mar-seille—the *généralité des garçons, compagnons, et ouvriers*—im-plies a series of distinctions in which differences in age, mari-tal status, and economic circumstance coexisted uneasily. It suggests a kind of balance among men whose concerns were not necessarily similar: young, single migrants or adolescents fresh from an apprenticeship (*garçons*); men who had served their time and expected to marry and acquire a *maîtrise* (*com-pagnons*); and men who were married, already settled, and probably relatively permanently engaged in journey work (*ouvriers*).

The ceremonial drinking and informal rituals of journey-men's associations are probably best understood in this con-text. They allowed journeymen to manage the passage of time: both from day to day, in the complex schedules of the things they did at work; and over the longer period, as the destinies of different people diverged substantially. The fact that the negotiation of difference became much more diffi-cult when the legal privileges and distinctive identity of the trades in Paris, Lyon, and Marseille began to disappear makes it possible to understand the subsequent violence be-tween rival journeymen's associations.

For most of the relatively long period covered by this es-say, the predominant concern of journeymen in the hatting trade was to use the courts to maintain what the law pre-scribed. Their attitude is of some relevance to recent discus-sion of flexible specialization, small businesses, and product

---

17. As has been mentioned, only 53 of a list of 274 journeymen (19 percent) working in the trade in Marseille shortly before 1789 were natives of the city or its diocese: A.C. Marseille, HH 399. On the composition of the trade in Lyon, see chapter 5.

diversification in the process of industrialization.[18] The eighteenth-century hatting trade was not impervious to technical change. Changes in materials and the manner of their preparation made it possible to respond to increases in the price of beaver by raising productive capacity. Thus, the trade might be added to the cases that have been cited as examples of the flexibility of artisanal enterprise. Yet that flexibility also entailed substantial changes in the relationship between the law and working conditions in the trade. The law, in other words, was more than an external presence that either favored or impeded innovation. It served to define the identities brought into play in the work of the trade and, at the same time, set limits on the integration of flexibility into established working arrangements. For the law was a part of those working arrangements. Eighteenth-century French journeymen did not live in a world bounded by esoteric ritual and exotic beliefs. Their culture was also the culture of the polity. The language they used and the claims they made were couched in the vocabulary of the law. The patterns of work that they followed were the product of the prevailing conventions of the law. Since the law implied that the hats they made were invested with their rights in their labor, they allocated the time they spent working in ways that ensured that the balance between what all of them did and what each of them made was common to working arrangements in each workshop.

These arrangements also met two objectives that were not a matter of discussion in the courts. The first was the daily cooperation required of pairs of journeymen, taken on individually for different periods of time. The second was the longer process of abandoning work for wages altogether, to find a place on the periphery of the trade. This aspect of the economy of the trade found little place in legal argument, although there is good reason to suppose that it was close to

18. See Charles Sabel and Jonathan Zeitlin, "Historical Alternatives to Mass Production: Politics, Markets, and Technology in Nineteenth-Century Industrialization," *Past and Present* 108 (1985): 133–76.

many journeymen's concerns. There was, for example, a sharp increase in the number of small hatting concerns that followed the abolition of the corporations in 1791. In his enumeration of the hatting trade of Lyon, Déglize noted that, although the size of the trade had fallen substantially (from 4,873 to 2,244 individuals) between 1789 and 1801, the number of enterprises had increased from 148 to 223, or by a little over 50 percent. Although the number of manufacturers or wholesalers producing on a scale large enough to warrant the employment of traveling salesmen had fallen from 70 to 58, the number of small manufacturers or retailers had increased from 78 to 165.[19] Despite the substantial reduction in the size of the trade (partly of course to the advantage of rural centers of production), small-scale enterprise on the periphery had an enduring and growing importance.

There were, in other words, concerns and preoccupations that were not embodied in the conventions of the law at all. They centered, in particular, upon the process of escaping from work for wages altogether. This aspect of the relationship between masters and journeymen has not, perhaps, been given the attention that it merits. Yet when the priors of the journeymen's confraternity in Marseille sought to emphasize the legitimate status of their association in 1716, they pointed to the fact that several of their number had subsequently been elected as the masters' own priors. Similarly, in 1721 one of the members of the Parisian confraternity pointed out that one of its treasurers was a master hatter.[20] Journeymen expected to become master hatters, if not large manufacturers.

It is unnecessary, in this context, to counterpose the vertical links between masters and journeymen to the lateral ties that existed among journeymen. The structure of the trade, with its central core and larger periphery, together with the possibilities it offered for subcontracted work, meant that work was also a process of accumulation that

19. A.C. Lyon, I² 46 bis, fol. 113.
20. See above, chapter 7.

depended upon certain forms of cooperation between masters and journeymen. That cooperation was linked to certain assumptions about—and entitlements to—employment, which found their expression in the somewhat ambivalent attitude of journeymen toward *alloués* and *dresseurs*. Journeymen refused to work with such outsiders but, as the rules devised by finishers in Lyon in 1776 indicate, were prepared to perform the same kind of work if it was available to their own kin. The dialogue between masters and journeymen was also a dialogue over the terms on which journeymen were able to abandon work for wages and begin to work on their own account. Much of that dialogue fell outside the prevailing conventions of the civil law, with its emphasis upon changes in formal status rather than changes in material circumstances.

Those conventions were modified under the pressure of two largely irreconcilable forces. The first was the pressure of the world market upon a relatively highly integrated branch of production. The growing scarcity of beaver fur resulted in the development of ways of preparing the fur of other animals to produce cheaper kinds of hats. The second was the enduring adherence of journeymen to working arrangements and practices that transcended the particularities of individual workshops or localities. Neither of these two forces (for want of a better word) was adequately acknowledged in the vocabulary and conventions of the law and public life. In the eyes of the journeymen, the pressure of the market was translated into the malevolent behavior of master hatters, represented by the use of shoddy materials, unqualified workers, and poisonous substances. In the eyes of the masters, the working practices of journeymen were translated into idleness, cupidity, and an endemic unwillingness to recognize the possibilities of higher productivity. In both cases, the particular preoccupations of each group were cast into, and strained against, the prevailing moral conventions of the natural law tradition of public discourse.

In argument of this kind, the situation of the journeymen

was the more vulnerable if only because, even during the first half of the eighteenth century, the conventions of public life allowed them little collective space. Although their associations enjoyed a large measure of toleration within the ambiguous netherworld of limited civil rights, their existence was never entirely free of undertones of clandestinity. Although their place in public life was recognized—in the form of processions on saints' days, funerals, and trade holidays—their identity derived as much from their capacity to challenge decisions by their masters' corporations in the courts as from more positive formal recognition. Even in Marseille, where the courts recognized the Luminaire de Sainte-Catherine de Sienne repeatedly until the last quarter of the eighteenth century, the *généralité* of journeymen in the trade had a shadowy and ambiguous status.

These ambiguities were an extension of the more fundamental ambiguity between the rights and obligations of producers in particular and the rights and obligations of society as a whole. As the breach between the two became wider, some of the ambiguities disappeared; by the 1780s the courts had made it clear that there was no place for the particular rights of journeymen in civic life. This position was very different from the more nuanced procedures that they had followed earlier. In 1736 a journeyman hatter in Marseille gave notice and then gravely inscribed a number of Latin words in chalk upon his employer's door. When translated, they announced that the master hatter in question, whose name was Bourgine, was not fit to have honest men work for him, even though some did.[21] The incident took place shortly before the same Bourgine and two other manufacturers appealed to the Parlement against a charge by the hatters' corporation that they had violated the provision of the statutes affecting the number of hats that could be made in a day. The court allowed the corporation to be joined in the proceedings by the priors of the journeymen's confraternity.

---

21. "Mr. Bourgine vous n'êtes pas capable d'avoir d'honnêtes gens chez vous, bien que vous en ayiez." A.C. Marseille, FF 342a (21 August 1736).

Nearly thirty years later the episode was cited as proof of the journeymen's title to the right to associate.[22]

These events are indicative of the way that, for much of the eighteenth century, interpersonal evaluation, acknowledgment of the rights and qualities of the individual producer, and the normative vocabulary of the law were not very distant. Even in 1785 and 1786, when many of their particular claims were no longer acknowledged, journeymen in Lyon and Paris were still able to take what amounted to collective legal action. By then, however, the notion that civil rights were the possession of those upon whom they had been conferred had given way to a simpler and more uniform manner of naming and defining rights. Yet many of the informal practices followed by journeymen's associations—their rules, trials, and fines in particular—continued to evoke the formal sanctions of the courts. The phrases used by journeymen in the late eighteenth and early nineteenth centuries—*fabriques en règle, le règlement de Paris*—were an acknowledgment of the idiom of a defunct legal process. By the early nineteenth century, however, these phrases had come to mean the measure of work in the trade. Their earlier associations with the law and the conventions of public life no longer existed. Legal precept had become traditional custom.

The tension between the rights of the producer and the claims of society has not disappeared. The history of an obscure eighteenth-century French trade suggests that the solution to that tension is not to be found entirely within the work that people do. For work itself is too heavily invested with meanings created elsewhere: in the courts, in the case of eighteenth-century France, and in the wider forums of public life. It is there—in the prevailing assumptions of a political culture—that the identity and significance of work are to be located and there, if anywhere, that its identity and significance might come to be informed by other and different notions of individual and collective rights.

22. A.D. Bouches-du-Rhône, B 4218 (17 October 1737). See also ibid., B 5633 (20 February 1764), where the case was cited as evidence of the journeymen's right to assemble.

A Note on Sources

Sources for the study of the urban trades of eighteenth-century France fall into three broad categories. The first group consists of the papers of the corporations to which most (but not all) master artisans belonged. Generally, they are housed in departmental archives as a subseries of the series E. The records of the hatters' corporations of Rouen (A.D. Seine-Maritime, 5E 204–11) and Toulouse (A.D. Haute-Garonne, E 1261–63) supplied some information about the relatively small trades of those two cities. The records of the hatters' corporations of Paris, Lyon, and Marseille have not survived. The papers of the Parisian corporation were destroyed, along with those of almost every other corporation, in 1871. Those of the hatters' corporations of Lyon and Marseille have also disappeared. Here, however, it is possible to overcome the difficulty because the minutes of corporate deliberations were also kept by their notaries.

The names of these notaries are relatively easy to find by referring to the registers of the *centième denier* (series 2C in departmental archives), which contain summary records of all eighteenth-century notarial transactions. These registers are, therefore, a convenient guide through the otherwise daunting mass of notarial records. Much of the information cited in this essay concerning corporate decisions in Lyon and Marseille has been based on the minutes of deliberations kept by the relevant notaries. They are housed in the appropriate subseries of the series E of the departmental archives of the Rhône and Bouches-du-Rhône. The minutes of one of the notaries of Marseille (A.D. Bouches-du-Rhône, 358E 201–25) also contain the record of the deliberations of the journeymen hatters' confraternity of the Luminaire de

Sainte-Catherine de Sienne. Specific references are supplied in the notes. Minutes of corporate deliberations were not, unfortunately, kept by Parisian notaries.

The second group of sources concerns the affairs of individual members of the trades. In the case of the hatting trade (and of most eighteenth-century urban trades), these sources fall into two categories: information on particular individuals contained in notarial records and information on particular hatting concerns contained mainly in bankruptcy records. Both types of sources present considerable problems of interpretation because of their inherent bias against ordinary prosperity and uneventful success. Notarial records capture individuals most frequently in early adulthood (when they married) or at the end of a career (when they made wills or when inventories were made of their assets). Bankruptcy records have even more obvious limitations. Neither source is an adequate substitute for a good collection of business records, which, in the case of the hatting trade, does not appear to have survived. Limited use has been made of both types of sources (located in series E of departmental archives, series D^5B^6 of the Archives de la ville de Paris and the Minutier central of the Archives nationales) for the information they contain on capital requirements, fixed costs, the prices of materials, and market structures.

The third category of sources, the records of the courts, have been used extensively in this essay. They fall into two broad groups. The first consists of the papers of those institutions that dealt with the affairs of the trades in the first instance: the Châtelet of Paris, the Consulat of Lyon, and the Echevinage of Marseille. The records of the branch of the Châtelet responsible for the trades, the Chambre de police, are located in the series Y of the Archives nationales. They are not complete and much of the information upon which decisions by the court were based has disappeared forever. Some of it, however, can be retrieved from the minutes of the *commissaires* of the Châtelet (whose papers make up the great bulk of the series Y). There are, however, almost insuperable obstacles to the location of all the information on a single trade that might lie among the huge mass of the papers of the *commissaires*. Very few of the *répertoires* of their minutes have survived, so that there is no general guide to the content of their papers. Some initial guidance can be found in four (very incomplete) collections of court rulings and police sentences: the Fonds Lamoignon housed in the Archives de la Préfecture de police, the Delamare and Dupuy collections housed in the Department of Manuscripts of the Bibliothèque nationale, and the Fonds Rondonneau of the Archives nationales (Series AD XI). Such rulings often present a summary of the preceding legal process, including the name of the *commissaire* to whom a formal complaint had been made and a reference to the relevant informations and depositions. Without such signals, research on particular trades in the minutes of the *commissaires* depends mainly upon reasoned guesswork and good fortune (in the proportions of 1 percent of the former to 99 percent of the latter, in my experience). As more historians explore the great wealth of information the minutes contain, much more is likely to be discovered.

The records of the municipal courts that dealt with the affairs of the trades in other cities have been divided between the series FF and series HH of municipal archives. The latter series was a nineteenth-century creation, which has both advantages and disadvantages. Documents that were submitted originally to either the Consulat of Lyon or the Echevinage of Marseille can now be found under the anachronistic rubric of the series HH, devoted to commerce and industry. They are therefore easy to find. Much of the surrounding documentation, however, is in the series FF, devoted to *police* and legal argument within the trades. In Lyon the series FF of the municipal archives has suffered substantially from this dismemberment, and the judicial records of the Consulat are therefore virtually nonexistent. In Marseille, however, the series FF is very full and, as specific notes in the text indicate, has supplied much information on disputes in the hatting trade there. There are, however, no detailed inventories of either series.

The second group of court records on which this essay has been based consists of the papers of the Parlements. The hatting trades of both Paris and Lyon fell within the jurisdiction of the Parlement of Paris, while that of Marseille fell under the Parlement of Provence. The papers of the Parlement of Paris are not easy to explore. There are, however, two valuable guides to research in Suzanne Clémencet et al., *Guide des recherches dans les fonds judiciaires de l'Ancien Régime* (Paris, 1958), and Madeleine Dillay, "Instruments de recherche du fonds du Parlement dressés au greffe de la juridiction," *Archives et bibliothèques* 3 (1937): 13–30, 82–92, 190–99. Most litigation involving the trades fell on the civil, rather than the criminal, side of the Parlement's activities, although assaults and seditious gatherings arising from disputes occasionally gave rise to appeals in the criminal division. A court ruling may therefore be found in any one of up to half a dozen different places within the voluminous collections of registers and minutes of the series X of the Archives nationales. Entry into the three series of civil *arrêts* (*conseil, plaidoiries,* and *jugés*) can be made by way of the registers of tables of civil *arrêts* (A.N. X^{1a} 9702–86). They are not, unfortunately, a complete record of *every* decision; they consist of a summary record of the procedural rulings made by the court that were issued to litigants and their lawyers before it reached its final verdict. As a result, they promise rather more than they deliver, and the researcher is again obliged to rely heavily on perseverance and good fortune. The Delamare, Dupuy, Lamoignon, and Rondonneau collections cited above provide some access to the *arrêts* and can be supplemented by the Joly de Fleury Collection housed in the Department of Manuscripts of the Bibliothèque nationale.

Much of the documentation on which this essay has been based was collected in the course of research on a wider study of the eighteenth-century French trades. This led to several discoveries, particularly among the manuscript collections of the municipal libraries of Lyon, Rouen, and Marseille and the Archives of the Chamber of Commerce of Marseille. Again, it is possible that there is much more to be found. The printed collections of French libraries and archives remain difficult to use as fully as might be possible were there a French equivalent to the admirable (and relatively well funded) *Eighteenth-Century Short Title Catalogue* produced by the British Library. Despite my best efforts, I was unable to locate a copy of a printed *factum* entitled "Précis sur la cause pour les compagnons chapeliers de la ville de Lyon contre les maîtres chapeliers de ladite ville" (Paris, 1761), cited by Roger Lecotté in his *Archives historiques du Compagnonnage* (Paris, 1951). Nor, despite much expenditure of time, was it possible to find any of the printed *factums* produced in the course of disputes in the hatting trade of Marseille and referred to in rulings by the Parlement of Provence.

These were not the only tantalizing hints of possible, but unrealized, discoveries. Edmond Soreau, in his "La Loi Le Chapelier," *Annales historiques de la Révolution française* 8 (1931): 287–314, wrote that in Paris in 1786 "les ouvriers du bâtiment soutiennent les chapeliers en grève par solidarité compagnonnique" (p. 290). Daniel Mornet, in his *Les Origines intellectuelles de la Révolution française* (5th ed., Paris, 1954), referred to a "strike" by Parisian hatters in 1778 (p. 448). Emile Coornaert, in a list of disputes in the Parisian trades appended to his *Les Compagnonnages en France* (Paris, 1966), noted disputes in the Parisian hatting trade in 1774, 1781, and 1782 (pp. 426–27). It is not possible to identify the sources on which these statements were based, nor, despite much effort, was it possible to confirm the existence of these reported events. There was, as has been shown, a dispute in the Parisian hatting trade in 1785, but there is nothing in the minutes of the *commissaires* concerning a stoppage by hatters in 1786. There were disputes in Lyon in 1774 and 1778 but not, to my knowledge, in Paris. Nor was it possible to find any trace of disputes in the Parisian hatting trade in either 1781 or 1782. More may come to light, because the huge resources of the papers of the Parlement of Paris have yet to reveal all they might contain. Even in this sense, the work of understanding the eighteenth-century French trades is still at a provisional stage.

A full bibliography in a book that is limited to a single trade but touches on a wide variety of different topics would be either pretentious or incomplete. The secondary works on the hatting trade, together with those of the most relevant authorities on the themes I have discussed, are indicated clearly in the footnotes to each chapter. As the statutes of the hatters' corporation of Marseille put it in 1716, it is "morally impossible" to do more.

Index

Compositor: Huron Valley Graphics
Text: 10/12 Palatino
Display: Palatino
Printer: Braun-Brumfield, Inc.
Binder: Braun-Brumfield, Inc.